Charles Maurice Davies

The Great Secret and its Unfoldment in Occultism

A Record of Forty Years' Experience in the Modern Mystery. Second Edition

Charles Maurice Davies

The Great Secret and its Unfoldment in Occultism
A Record of Forty Years' Experience in the Modern Mystery. Second Edition

ISBN/EAN: 9783337267360

Printed in Europe, USA, Canada, Australia, Japan

Cover: Foto ©Lupo / pixelio.de

More available books at **www.hansebooks.com**

ANNA KINGSFORD:

HER LIFE, LETTERS, AND WORK.

BY HER COLLABORATOR,

EDWARD MAITLAND.

Illustrated with Portraits, Views, Facsimiles, &c. 2 vols.
Demy 8vo, 896 pp., cloth. 31s. 6d. net.

Being a record of the extraordinary experiences in virtue of which they were enabled to produce "The Perfect Way," and the other books which have found high recognition with students of Spiritual Science, this book will be of the greatest interest and importance to all serious inquirers. While, in comprising, as it does, the evidences on which they relied for their restoration of the long-lost doctrine of the soul's pre-existence, the multiplicity of the earth-lives necessary for its evolution and final regeneration, and its power to recover, in a later incarnation, the memory of knowledges acquired and experiences undergone in its earlier incarnations—which evidences are founded on their own personal experience—it is a book wholly unique, and will be a contribution of unapproached value to the philosophy of existence. The nature of the narrative also is such as to give it, even for the general reader, an interest far surpassing that of any mere romance.

Crown 8vo, 350 pp., cloth. 5s. net.

A RELIGION OF LAW:

BEING THE CONCLUSIONS OF A STUDENT OF PSYCHIC FACTS.

By V. C. DESERTIS.

PART I
THE BASIS OF EXPERIMENTAL FACT.

CHAPTER I.—THE PHYSICAL PHENOMENA, OR OUTWARD FACTS, THE EVIDENCE OF THE SENSES. CHAPTER II.—THE INNER OR SUBJECTIVE FACTS—MEDIUMSHIP. CHAPTER III.—THE MORALITY OF "SPIRITUALISM."

PART II
THEORY AND INFERENCES.

CHAPTER I.—MATTER AND ETHER. CHAPTER II.—THE ORDERS OF EXISTENCE. CHAPTER III.—THE GATE OF DEATH. CHAPTER IV.—BODY—THE MEANS OF ACTION. CHAPTER V.—SOUL—THE FORMING POWER. CHAPTER VI.—SPIRIT—THE DIRECTING WILL. CHAPTER VII.—THE HUMAN FAMILY.

THE
GREAT SECRET

CAN THIS BE DEATH?

"I HAD a dream. Methought I saw the Soul,
   With all her grand affections full in bloom,
   High thoughts and noble aims. Upon the tomb
She stood on tiptoe. Meekness marked the whole
Of her sublime devotion. On the goal
   Of life she gazed—of life in amplest room,
   Replete with wonders and exempt from gloom.
Then nearer to her rosy feet I stole,
And found the tomb a corpse of fairest mould,
   The unlike likeness of the Soul—so pale,
So motionless, and growing deadly cold.
   Some instinct would not let my heart bewail.
   The Soul was mounting slowly. *She* was hale,
And in immortal youth already old."

—J. C. EARLE.

THE GREAT SECRET

AND ITS UNFOLDMENT IN OCCULTISM

A RECORD OF FORTY YEARS' EXPERIENCE
IN THE MODERN MYSTERY

BY

A CHURCH OF ENGLAND CLERGYMAN

"If a man die, shall he live again?"

SECOND EDITION

LONDON
GEORGE REDWAY
1896

CONTENTS

CHAP.		PAGE
I.	INTRODUCTORY. A WAVE OF SUPERNATURALISM	1
II.	THE JUDGMENT OF PARIS	15
III.	IN STATU PUPILLARI	48
IV.	THE HYPNOTIC BORDERLAND	63
V.	IN THE HANDS OF THE MASTERS	93
VI.	OCCULTISM IN ITS HOMELY ASPECTS	125
VII.	MRS. GRUNDY'S ANATHEMA	158
VIII.	STUDYING THE STARS	189
IX.	FROM SPIRIT TO MATTER	211
X.	MYSTERIES IN MAYFAIR	229
XI.	A MYSTIC ORATORY	252
XII.	THE MEANING OF A MYSTICAL SERVICE	269
XIII.	THE WAVE SUBSIDING. CONCLUSION	283
	POSTSCRIPT	307

THE GREAT SECRET

CHAPTER I

A WAVE OF SUPERNATURALISM

"Suave, mari magno turbantibus æquora ventis,
E terrâ magnam alterius spectare laborem;
Non quia vexari quenquam est jucunda voluptas,
Sed quibus ipse malis careas quia cernere suave est.
. . . .
O miseras hominum mentes, O pectora cæca!
Qualibus in tenebris vitæ quantisque periclis
Degitur hoc ævi quodcumque est!"   —LUCRETIUS.

"'Tis sweet to stand upon some peaceful shore
While winds are whistling, and while billows roar;
And from that vantage-ground serenely see
Folks filled with fears from which ourselves are free.
. . . .
O hapless mind of man, with blindness rife!
How overshadowed is the span of life,
Brief though it be!"   —*M.S. Translation.*

WHEN the subject of this volume was suggested to me, the question at once occurred, should it be cast in the form of a personal narrative pure and simple; or should it be a record of things heard and seen, in the sense of including what might be deemed trustworthy evidence at second hand?

Without at all disparaging the value of such evidence, or resolving to forego its occasional aid, I felt very strongly that the narrative must be in the first place essentially personal. I know from long experience how difficult it is to persuade outsiders that you have really witnessed what you set down for their acceptance, and how enormously that difficulty is increased by every step which removes you from the original experience. The ideal at which I aim is this—to be able to say to my readers: "I have witnessed such and such phenomena"—not that somebody else told me they had witnessed them. "I have seen, heard, or felt certain things which, so far as I can see, lie outside the range of our ordinary experiences; and I tell you as clearly as I can the conditions under which those effects were produced, in order that you may set to work and reproduce them for yourselves. Nothing short of this will beget in you that faith which alone deserves the name, and which I define as *conviction based on adequate evidence.* Anything short of this is credulity. Even when this is presented to you at first hand, you have to shake yourself well and pull yourself together so as to be quite sure you are not led away through the tricks of 'strong imagination.' I have gone through all this ordeal myself, and feeling sure you will have to do the same, I want to save you as much trouble as possible, specially in the way of diminishing the distance of your point of view from the original experience."

Of course the adoption of this form involves a more copious use of the first personal pronoun than a modest man likes; but this diffidence must be overcome if it be desired to inspire confidence in one's readers.

Were the matter at issue a small or unimportant one, it would be possible to feel less keenly on the subject; but from a comparatively early period my own examination of the Modern Mystery assumed the form of an inquiry into the evidence for immortality. It was either that or nothing; at best a silly pastime not worth occupying the attention of a rational man. It proposed to solve the Great Secret; to answer Job's question, "If a man die, shall he live again?" not by an appeal to Church or Scripture, or any form of revelation hitherto comprised under that name, but by an appeal to sight and sense. It was a bold position to assume—a "large order," as the modern phrase goes, to execute; and nothing short of a personal narrative would be adequate, even if that should be deemed sufficient.

I venture to claim a hearing, then, first of all on account of the gravity of my subject. Can immortality be proved by occult science? Is the survival of the entire personality after the temporary shock of dissolution through death in any degree demonstrable? It is the supreme question which every one must ask, the single great secret in the solution of which we are all equally interested. And I claim the right, too, because I have devoted so many years of my life to that solution. In the nature of things, I must soon solve the question experimentally for myself; and I should like, before I pass out into the darkness, to leave on record, as completely as may be, my gropings towards the light.

A third claim for hearing might fairly enough be put forward; though, for obvious reasons, I shall not dwell upon it at any length at present. It is this. Although, as I have said, this new evidence promised to supersede that of Church or Bible, yet there was in it nothing at all antagonistic to these accustomed channels of revelation. It was, as I saw from the first, supplementary to the old evidence. Later on, I got to see that the new was but a development of the old; but it would be an anachronism and an anticipation of the sequel were I to dwell on this aspect of my subject at present. I therefore only mention it in passing.

On the vexed question of anonymity there is something to be said pro and con. After duly weighing the arguments on both sides, I have come to the conclusion that the official—shall we say "professional"?—title is of more importance than the personal. The bulk of our criticism is anonymous; and perhaps we should not think so highly of it if the critics always appended their names. I have determined, therefore, to follow their example. I am sure my name would not add weight to my remarks, while the statement of my clerical calling warns my readers what kind of criticism they may expect.

As to whether I am the proper person to offer such a solution as is now contemplated to the Great Question, I can only say that I have assumed the task after long hesitation and anxious consideration; and the matter seems to me to stand thus: many persons look into occultism for their personal satisfaction, but keep their own counsel as to the result of their observation. They put nothing on record to help others. It would be hard to call this a conspiracy of silence, because there are many less questionable reasons for reluctance to speak. I should be only too glad to be silent; but I feel that some one ought to speak. I am quite willing to concede that there are many more capable men than myself for such a task as I propose—scientific men, for example, who are accustomed to search into the mysteries of nature, or legal authorities whose business it has been to weigh evidence; but, with such honourable exceptions as Professor Crookes on the one side, and the late Sergeant Cox on the other, I know of few persons who have kept persistently "pegging away" at the subject for so long a period as myself; so let my evidence be taken for what it is worth.

On the score of personal fitness, I believe

I am not destitute of a proper modicum of diffidence; and I am sure I tried, during my investigations, to keep my eyes and ears well open, while my tongue was still. It was with considerable pleasure, therefore, that I came upon a passage in a book with the author of which I am quite unacquainted; but he was so good as to say that if the evidence for some of these occult matters convinced a hard-headed person like myself (naming me as the author of a certain work published some years ago), that evidence was good enough for him.

I do not know that I can claim hard-headedness as my special characteristic; nor am I at all inclined to pose as a "superior person" in any way. I have simply brought to bear on this matter such intelligence as I could command, "be the same," as the lawyers say, "more or less." I had no theory to back up, or prejudices that I wished to bolster, parson though I am. I was free from all bias when I commenced my investigations; nor am I now anxious to offer my convictions, such as they are, for the acceptance of others. I state those convictions fully and frankly, and leave others to appraise them at their proper value. What I consider of far greater importance than any theories is the accumulation of facts in almost every branch of occult study extending over many years. I have given pretty well an average lifetime to the collection of evidence, and now I sum it up, leaving the verdict to my readers. I am not an advocate pro or con; nor is my narrative intended to be in any sense an apologia.

It was for this reason, again, I preferred to make that narrative almost exclusively a personal one. I felt that whilst a few slipshod readers might wish me to assume infallibility, and offer them cut and dried conclusions, the great majority of capable inquirers would prefer that I should give them hard facts, and leave them to draw their conclusions for themselves. I do not for one moment wish to shirk the responsibility of my opinions; but, so far as my possible readers are concerned, I am well aware that my judgment, on the whole question or on any branch of it, may not, and probably will not, be theirs.

I have nothing to gain or lose by the frank enunciation of my views or the recapitulation of my experiences. The orthodox have dubbed me heretical for touching a tabooed topic; the infallible people have deemed me — well, anything but "hard-headed," because I coquetted so constantly with what they decided off-hand was only a delusion and a fraud. Even my own familiar friends in whom I trusted smiled indulgently at my proclivities for "hocus-pocus." Perhaps these different attitudes have had the effect of making me reticent in the past; but, I repeat, I have nothing to gain or to lose by outspokenness now. It may be taken for granted, then, that what I here set down represents my own genuine opinion, and the result of my own unbiassed observation, whatever that may be worth.

By the large number of persons who claim to monopolise the title of occultists I have been ever regarded as lukewarm and Laodicean, because I have worn no badge and belonged to no "party." The fact is, I have always regarded the word "spiritualist" as what Archbishop Whately called a "question-begging" one. I have never used it myself, and shall omit it from my narrative, save when I use it on compulsion. Whenever I have been asked whether I was a Spiritualist, I have answered by asking for a definition of the term; and then I have been accused of fencing with the question.

A tidal wave of Supernaturalism—so-called—had risen on the other side of the Atlantic some score of years before I began my investigations. It was cresting on our shores when I commenced. I was fortunate, therefore, in my opportunity; for the wave seems to have subsided again. People complain that there are no facilities for occult study now; but there was no difficulty then. I fancy it is only the form of occultism that has changed. The thing is amongst us still; but its shapes are Protean, and there is no likelihood of their being exhausted.

I spoke just now of "so-called" Supernaturalism. The term is a misleading one, because it confounds nature with our knowledge of nature. Whatever the source—or sources—of all these different manifestations, they are, no doubt, purely natural, though they carry us into a domain of law with which we are at present unacquainted or but partially familiarised. This is the view taken by Professor Drummond in his engrossing work, "Natural Law in the Spiritual World." It is, to some extent, the view of Isaac Taylor, too, in his "Physical Theory of Another Life." This latter book was written before the Modern Mystery came to the front, and is on that account the more interesting, because it touches our present subject at more than one point of contact. One of his most striking hypotheses is that the sphere which we at present inhabit may possibly be conterminous with the outer fringe of the spiritual world. But even so, the one would be as purely natural as the other. The material and the spiritual planes may not be so diametrically opposed as some of us think; since it is impossible with our present faculties to conceive spirit apart from some kind of matter, however attenuated. It is better, therefore, to eliminate the word "supernatural" from our vocabulary. It really involves something like a contradiction of terms, and accordingly I use it under protest, and by way of accommodation to prevalent ideas, just as we speak of the sun rising and setting without expressing any disbelief in the heliocentric system.

The word "occultism" seems to suit all purposes. It expresses our present ignorance, whilst it leaves room for hope that what is now occult may one day be revealed.

What, in fact, is all that follows but such a partial unfoldment of the occult, such a supplementary revelation of something that else might be hidden, touching more especially on that one point which Bible and Church veil so cautiously, and which Paganism and Christianity, with similar modesty, have elected to name Hades—the Unseen World?

CHAPTER II

THE JUDGMENT OF PARIS

> "This was your motive
> For Paris, was it? Speak."
> —SHAKESPEARE, *All's Well that
> Ends Well*, i. 3.

DELIBERATELY and of set purpose do I venture on the play of words involved in the heading of this chapter, because I want to protest at the very outset against the grim style adopted by nearly all my predecessors when dealing with any branch of this subject. They are terribly in earnest, of course, and therefore feel bound to treat everything *au sérieux*. I have chosen the serious side of my subject too; but I cannot forget that this subject has a grotesque—one might almost say a comic—side as well; and the presentation of it would be incomplete if we did not take in all the details. But the occultist is, for the most part, thin-skinned, and resents any sort of trifling. He forgets that Dante called his colossal work not the Divine Tragedy, but the Divine Comedy.

The opening scene of my drama lies in Paris; and we sad and insular English people are apt to regard Paris only as the gay metropolis to which we resort as a distraction from our own gloomy fatherland. We too frequently forget that life in Paris has its serious side as well—its shadow along with its sunshine. It was to a very serious phase of Parisian existence my attention was turned when, in the autumn of 1856, I took up my residence in a street of the English quarter, some portion of which has since, I fancy, been Haussmannised off the face of the great world of Paris; at least I have never been able to find my former residence, in any of my subsequent visits.

The days of the Second Empire were then

in their infancy; and so was the little Prince Imperial, who used to be frequently borne forth by his buxom peasant nurse for the benefit of admiring crowds in the Tuileries Gardens, while his imperial papa smoked his cigar on the terrace. It seems as though one were indeed writing about some previous phase of existence, seeing that father and son have been in their graves for so many years, and the palace is but the shadow of its former self. Even then, Paris was beginning to feel constitutionally antique; for events move quickly in France, while the changes are for the most part sudden and violent. Paris in 1856 needed a new sensation; so, as the social and political world were fairly quiet just then, she turned her attention to the suprasensual and the transcendental spheres. She set herself to prove immortality by occultism.

That gifted seer with the Scottish name and the American nationality, Daniel Dunglass Home, had been holding frequent seances at the Tuileries;[1] and since the secrets of the palace were not so closely "tiled" in Paris as in London, we common people were able to hear blood-curdling accounts as to how the First Napoleon showed his spectral hand in the darkened chamber, and wrote his familiar signature full in front of the amazed spectators. Our flesh was continually "creeping" at such recitals.

I say "we" common people, because I had transformed myself for the time being into a Parisian citizen. I had recently vacated my academical fellowship by entering on one of a matrimonial character; and after a brief period of hotel existence on the Continent, my wife and myself had come to the conclusion that Paris would be a very nice place for a temporary residence

---

[1] There is some confusion of date in Home's "Incidents in My Life," with regard to these Parisian manifestations. In his life written by his wife she refers to certain events which took place at Paris in 1856, "which," she says, "Home referred to in his 'Incidents,' but mistakenly gave the date as 1857."

at all events. I am not at all sure that
the ghostly doings at the Tuileries and
their repetition elsewhere had not some
attractive power in them; anyhow, as I had
no duties, lay or clerical, to call me back
to England, I put half-a-dozen trial advertisements into *Galignani's Messenger* intimating
my willingness to instruct the ingenuous
youth of Paris either in ancient classics or
in modern English.

Strangely enough, my half-dozen advertisements brought me exactly the same number
of engagements, which were as many as I
wanted, and more than I expected. My
pupils were respectively a French marquis
who had married the daughter of an English
banker in Paris, and wanted to be able to
talk to his wife; a young Pole, Kierzkowski,
whose ambition was to qualify for Woolwich
and enter the English artillery; a young
Oxford student whom we designated familiarly
"Sammy Smith;" three boys—here grouped
as one—sons of a globe-trotting physician

temporarily settled in Paris; and last, though far from least, two young ladies—whom I do not bracket together, because they studied separately—one being a sister of the marquise above mentioned and daughter of the English banker, and the other her cousin, who afterwards continued her English studies with me in London, and whose brother passed from my hands into the army, not without some difficulty, since his polyglot education in various Continental cities produced the same condition of chaos in his mind as was brought about of old in the builders of Babel. I mention this youth here, though he is a little out of date, because, as will be seen by-and-by, he played a subsidiary part in my occult studies.

Here, then, almost before I was aware of it, I settled down into my temporary Parisian citizenship. We took a little furnished apartment *au troisième* in the Rue des Ecuries d'Artois. It consisted of the orthodox five "pieces"—salle-à-manger, salon, two bedrooms and kitchen, all of which could have been packed comfortably into one room of a moderately-sized villa in a London suburb.

The second sleeping-room was meant for a servant; but as we did not indulge in that luxury at first—our concierge doing what was necessary in our modest ménage—it was occupied by the lady to whom the apartment belonged, who was a former governess of my wife, and was then engaged as a visiting governess in Paris. She too, though by no means *spirituelle*, played a part in our subsequent studies of supramundane phenomena. We should never have dreamed of putting anything larger than a cat or a toy-terrier to sleep in that room, which was scarcely more than a good-sized cupboard; but our "landlady" managed to screw herself into it somehow, and appeared to enjoy her slumbers there.

I mention all these apparently trivial details of our Parisian existence, as well as other autobiographical passages which seem without relevance to our occult experiences, because I want to impress on my readers how entirely those experiences came to me in the ordinary course of events. I did not approach my subject with any strong preconceived opinions. I did not seek it out; but it sought me. It is the unexpected that always happens; and nothing seemed less likely than that a year's residence in Paris by a newly-married young parson should prove for him the borderland of the occult. Such, however, was the case. Those séances at the Tuileries had set Paris talking. It does not take much to do that; but they also set Paris experimenting. "Circles" were formed for the purpose of reproducing those imperial experiences. That was the gay Parisian form which the grand question of immortality assumed. Theology was henceforth to become a fixed science, and the survival of the personality was to be proved like a theorem in Euclid, with a Q.E.D. at the end. Under the circumstances, and looking at the subject from the vantage-ground of the present, it appears to me that, instead of rushing madly into the matter, we displayed a more than usual amount of British hesitation and tardiness. The miracle was that the gimcrack tables of our little salon in the Rue des Ecuries d'Artois did not begin pirouetting sooner than was actually the case.

They commenced in due course; but the impetus certainly did not emanate from ourselves. The contagion reached us from outside. Personally I knew nothing at that time of "the Modern Mystery," which had been imported from America and had taken firm root in English soil so many years before. Afterwards I became familiarly acquainted with the heroine of the "Rochester Knockings," but I had never heard of her or of them then. I had once seen a table careering about in a drawing-room amid a laughing group, and thought the phenomenon a curious one, if not a clever trick; just as I did when four girls lifted my tolerably bulky form on the tips of their fingers from the table on which it was extended, by following the directions given in Sir David Brewster's " Natural Magic." They only let me fall when we could no longer hold our breath for laughter; but I never dreamed of connecting a serious thought with either of these table-traits, and Sir David himself would never "give in," as he phrased it, to any occult explanation of the otherwise inexplicable phenomena. Now, however, I was bidden by Parisian society, in its temporarily serious phase, to accept these tabular gyrations as, so to say, the alphabet of immortality.

The time for my "conversion" had not yet come; but it was a good deal nearer than I thought. What is a conversion worth if it does not take you by surprise?

That young governess who slept in our corner cupboard became a most important link in the chain of events. I was the more glad to have secured her presence, because I now added to my tutorial duties those of

Paris correspondent to a London weekly paper. The quest of gossip necessitated my frequent absence from home; and I was delighted to have found a companion for my wife, who thus became the recipient of marvellous stories about the *diablerie* occurring in private circles among the families where our juvenile landlady had pupils. Madame Blank had received undoubted proof that her departed husband was still with her; and Monsieur Asterisk had been favoured with information which could have emanated from none but his deceased grandparent. I laughed at it all, and refused to dignify it even with the ill-omened title of *diablerie*, which rather expressed the theory of our Lady of the Corner Cupboard, but which appeared to me to beg the whole question at issue. I could find nothing more appropriate than the contemptuous terms, "hocus-pocus" or "hanky-panky," for was I not as yet unconverted? For a long time I went on serenely with my Greek plays and English conversations, and let "the women" talk.

Like Paris in general, however, these good ladies were not content with talking; they experimented too. It was discovered that my wife possessed the gift of automatic writing. If she held a pen or pencil in her hand, that is, and exercised no conscious control over it, words would be written, and answers given to questions "uttered or unexpressed." I say no *conscious* control, because I am anxious not to beg the question; and it is only fair to the automatic writer in this case, to say that she herself never felt satisfied with this method of communication, and never exercises her gift—for it remains with her still—except under the strongest possible pressure. She was even then fully satisfied that her own volition had nothing to do with bringing about the result; but she felt, and still feels, the difficulty of convincing others that such can be the case.

All this I was *told;* but I was, for the time being, a Gallio, and cared for none of these things. My conversion was yet to come, and I little dreamed how close I was then standing upon the threshold of the occult. The event came about in the following manner.

Circumstances seemed at this time as though they combined to force the subject of occultism upon me; though, so far from seeking it, I rather held myself studiously aloof from it, as I wanted to keep a cool head in order to devote myself to my somewhat numerous duties. But it was not so to be.

Certainly Paris was a thorough workshop for me. They begin studies early there. Young Kierzkowski used to come for a lesson at 7 A.M., and he had caught the ghost-fever like the rest. Then I would sally forth, after an early cup of coffee, for an hour's reading and conversation with my marquis. Of course he insisted on commencing his

English reading with the most idiomatic parts of Charles Dickens, and was greatly disappointed to find his dictionary gave him no clue as to what "alley tors and commoneys" were in the Bardell v. Pickwick case. He kept a pack of hounds at his country place, and I had to help him write horsey and doggy letters to people in England. These matters were almost as mysterious to me as Master Bardell's marbles were to the marquis, or the New Revelation to people in general. Here, however, the subject of the occult was tabooed, for the family were rigid Catholics, and deemed all ghostly subjects to be dealings with the devil. This always appeared to me the most advanced pneumatology possible, since it not only decided that "spirits" were at work, but even identified the communicating intelligence. Then Sammy Smith would come and wail through a Greek chorus, giving my wife, who listened in an adjoining room, the idea that a Greek drama consisted mainly of interjections.

After this, the boys would come, or I would go to my lady pupils; and after dejeuner I was free for the collection of Parisian gossip.

Soon after we had settled down into our new life, one of my brothers paid us a visit. He was not by any means a transcendental person, and knew little more of the Modern Mystery than I did myself. Just before he left England, however, he had been present at one of the séances in the house of Dr. Rymer at Ealing. It was here, I believe, that the manifestations subsequently occurred which formed the subject of the article in the *Cornhill Magazine* in August 1860, under the title of "Truth stranger than Fiction."

The article commenced as follows, and I cannot do better than place the words thus in the forefront of my own story, because they represent with sufficient accuracy my own attitude on this question:—

"'I have seen what I would not have

believed on your testimony, and what I cannot, therefore, expect you to believe on mine,' was the reply of Dr. Treviranus to inquiries put to him by Coleridge as to the reality of certain magnetic phenomena which that distinguished savant was reported to have witnessed. It appears to me that I cannot do better than adopt this answer as an introduction to the narrative of facts I am about to relate. It represents very clearly the condition of the mind before and after it has passed through experiences of things that are irreconcilable with known laws. I refuse to believe such things upon the evidence of other people's eyes; and I even possibly go so far as to protest that I would not believe them even on the evidence of my own. When I have seen them, however, I am compelled to regard the subject from an entirely different point of view. It is no longer a question of mere credence or authority, but a question of fact. Whatever conclusions, if any, I may have arrived at on this question of fact, I see distinctly that I have been projected into a better position for judging of it than I occupied before, and that what then appeared an imposition, or a delusion, now assumes a shape which demands investigation. But I cannot expect persons who have not witnessed these things to take my word for them, because, under similar circumstances, I certainly should not have taken theirs. What I do expect is, that they will admit as reasonable, and as being in strict accordance with the philosophical method of procedure, the mental progress I have indicated, from the total rejection of extraordinary phenomena upon the evidence of others, to the recognition of such phenomena, as matter of fact, upon our own direct observation. This recognition points the way to inquiry, which is precisely what I desire to promote."

It is now an open secret that the article was written by Robert Bell. Its insertion, I fancy, created some temporary odium against Thackeray, who then edited the *Cornhill*, and who was thought to have offered a kind of premium on charlatanism by admitting the narrative into the pages of a respectable periodical; for even then the goblins were not held to be of good repute. Indeed Thackeray himself seemed to anticipate some such objections, since he appends the following editorial note: "As Editor of this Magazine, I can vouch for the good faith and honourable character of our correspondent, a friend of twenty-five years' standing; but as the writer of the above astounding narrative owns that he 'would refuse to believe such things upon the evidence of other people's eyes,' his readers are therefore free to give or withhold their belief.—ED."

It is an ungallant confession to make, no doubt, but it is true nevertheless, that I paid more attention to the fraternal narrative of hocus-pocus than I did to the reiterated stories told by my wife and her companion.

I even consented to "sit" and see whether we could reproduce any of the marvellous phenomena which were alleged to have taken place at Ealing. I yielded under protest; but my brother put it so persuasively that I should have been pigheaded had I refused.

"Very likely nothing will occur," he urged; "but our time is not particularly valuable; so we may as well try."

Then we "sat."

We were four in number—myself, my brother, my wife, and young Kierzkowski. If he is now a bronzed veteran and reads these words, he will be amused to find his early experiences thus put on record.

The table soon began to spin merrily; and here a strange phenomenon occurred, seeming to militate against any theory of involuntary muscular action, which was, as I knew, Faraday's rationale of the process. The table was one of those gimcrack French affairs that for the most part have something wrong with their works. The worm of the screw was worn out, so that if you pressed the table, the top twisted on the slightest provocation, and no amount of pressure would move the legs; but when it turned under our process of hanky-panky, it spun round *legs and all!* This was really the first step in my conversion. That table was forthwith metamorphosed for me into a kind of Delphic tripod.

Then it answered questions, tilting, by previous arrangement, three times for "yes," once for "no," twice if the reply was doubtful, or five times if it wished us to repeat the alphabet, when it would lift under our hands at the letter required, and thus laboriously spell out sentences.

Still clinging to my scepticism, I hazarded a conjecture that we were doing all this ourselves—that is, I enunciated the theory of unconscious cerebration, which was the other part of Faraday's explanation.

Then my brother, who was showman on

the occasion, told me to go to a side-table, write any question I liked, keeping it carefully concealed, and wait for a reply. I wrote as follows:

By what power is the table moved?

Slowly, as some child at a dame's school, that Delphic table commenced its reply:

To the spirits of the departed this power is given——

Here, by way of test, I was rude enough to interrupt, and "cut in" with another query, giving no intimation that I had done so:

What is the use of it?

To my utilitarian demand came the rejoinder:

IT MAY MAKE MEN BELIEVE IN GOD.

Here, I confess, I struck my colours. I was not near the table, and those who were sitting at it could have no idea what I was asking. I might have inquired the number of coins in my pocket, or how many books there were on the shelves. The answers were intelligent, and fitted my questions. I would put one more, which could admit of no vagueness in the answer:

What was the nickname we called R. B. (naming a deceased friend) *at college?*

Peepy.

Now, this nickname, be it remarked, was utterly unknown to all present except myself. I was not at the table when it was given, nor did I mention what I had written. The circuitous method of explanation now called "telepathy" had not then been devised; or, if it had, I had certainly never heard of it, nor can I even now see how it could have been pressed into our service on this occasion.

Then I was "converted." They tell me my face was a treat to see, so complete was my mystification. I saw, at all events, there was "something in it." Remember, the days of thought-reading were not as yet. What could I do but accept facts forced thus against my will upon me, and resolve to find out the underlying theory if possible?

Forthwith our little French apartment became a miniature shrine of Delphi or Dodona. Sealed envelopes were sent in, containing questions to be answered in automatic writing by my wife. The answers were, in all cases which were reported, declared to be absolutely correct. But I had no opportunity of checking this assertion; and considering the excitement which prevailed at the time, and the propensity of the average Parisian inquirer, I was not inclined to build very much on this basis.

Far more satisfactory were the little private confabs which my wife and myself used to have à deux with the self-styled "intelligences." I laughed still, despite my recent conversion, when they told us that we were named in the spheres according to our moral qualities, and that my name was Thomas, which meant, "Not steadfast in the faith," while hers was Mary, and this signified, "Not seeing, but believing." I verily believe this was a misnomer, for I think I believed more than she did just then. I believed in her, but she was doubtful of herself. She always was—and, indeed, is to the present day—afraid lest she might be unconsciously controlling the pencil or pen, and simply writing down her own ideas.

But ever and anon there came communications which, for the time, at all events, dispelled her doubts, and dissipated my mirth. I mention one case of this kind by way of example.

Looking forward to our future permanent settlement in England, I kept my eyes open for any appointment which might suit the scholastic turn my tastes had taken, without interfering with my clerical pursuits, to which I still clung. A vacancy occurred in the staff of masters at my old school—King's College—and I wrote to the secretary, with whom I had some personal acquaintance, suggesting that I should like to become a candidate. He thought well of my chances of success, and advised me strongly to come over and offer myself for the appointment, which I resolved to do.

Now, our unseen guides had always sternly refused to tell us anything about the future. "It could," they said, "only make man's life one of unceasing misery if he knew exactly the fate that awaited him." They therefore refused to say one word as to my success in the proposed candidature.

"But," I suggested, "you might at least tell me what form the election will take."

"From the general body of candidates," they replied, "three will be selected; and from these three one will be chosen for final election."

"There, now!" I exclaimed, feeling, no doubt, very clever at having caught my guides tripping, "you have broken your own rule. You *have* told us something about the future."

"No," was the instant reply, "we have not. The form of election is already settled by the electors."

This is by no means the most striking instance I shall have to give of cases where the communication crossed, as it were, the calculations of those through whom they came, and thus appeared to do away with the theory of unconscious muscular action plus thought-reading.

As I have alluded, however, to these theories, it may be well—though possibly inartistic—to set down here what had so far been formulated on the subject.

In the *Athenæum* for 2nd June 1853 is a long communication from Professor Faraday giving full particulars of his "Experimental Investigation of Table-Moving," the result of which was, he came to the conclusion "there was nothing in it" beyond involuntary muscular action. "The communication," says the *Athenæum*, "is of great importance in the present morbid condition of public thought —when, as Professor Faraday says, the effect produced by table-turners has, without due inquiry, been referred to electricity, to magnetism, to attraction, to some unknown or hitherto unrecognised physical power able to affect inanimate bodies, to the revolution of the earth, and even to diabolical or supernatural agency. . . . 'I have been,' says the Professor, 'greatly startled by the revelation which *this purely physical subject* has made of the public mind. No doubt there are many persons who have formed a right judgment or used a cautious reserve, for I know several such, and public communications have shown it to be so; but their number is almost as nothing to the great body who have believed and borne testimony, as I think, in the cause of error.'"

This quotation is made by the *Athenæum* from a previous letter to the *Times;* and it shows that Professor Faraday's opinion of the British public might have been expressed in Mr. Bumble's historic words, namely, that it was "a ass!"

After three full columns of descriptive matter, the Professor concludes: "I must bring this long description to a close. I am a little ashamed of it; for I think, in the present age, and in this part of the world, it ought not to have been required. . . . Finally, I beg to direct attention to the discourse delivered by Dr. Carpenter at the Royal Institution on the 12th of March 1852, entitled 'On the Influence of Suggestion in modifying and directing Muscular Movement, independently of Volition,' which, especially in the latter part, should be considered in reference to table-moving, by all who are interested in the subject."

Dr. Carpenter's views may be conveniently gathered from his work on "Mental Physiology," p. 632. He says :—

"It has happened over and over again in the writer's experience that what *he* considered as simple facts, admitting a perfectly natural explanation, were interpreted as the results of some occult agency, Mesmeric or Spiritual as the case might be. And from these cases the transition is easy to others in which subjective sensations are referred to objective realities. Thus, when two spiritualistic performers, in perfectly good faith, asserted that a table rose from the floor beneath their hands, whilst a third person, who was carefully watching the feet of the table, declared that one of them had never left the ground, it turned out that the first assertion entirely rested upon their mental conviction that they had 'felt it pressing upwards against their hands'—a tactile sensation obviously producible by their expectation of such an occurrence. And so, when Mr. Varley assures us that he has seen, in broad daylight, a large dining-table lifted bodily off the floor, and moved in the direction which he mentally requested it to take, we have to consider whether it is more consistent with inherent probability that Mr. Varley interpreted subjective visual perceptions produced by his mental expectation as objective realities, or that the table was actually raised, either by his own 'psychic force' or by the agency of disembodied spirits (*Quarterly Review*, October 1871, pp. 330, 348). The process by which the mind of a person given up to the 'possession' of dominant ideas is first led to *misinterpret actual occurrences*, and then (as in dreams) to *invent objective* explanations of his *own sensations*, is perfectly familiar to all who have studied the phenomena of insanity. And every one who accepts as facts, merely on the evidence of his senses, or on the testimony of others who partake of his own beliefs, what Common Sense tells him to be much more probably the fiction of his own imagination—even though confirmed by the testimony of hundreds affected with the same epidemic delusion—must be regarded as the subject of a 'diluted insanity.'"

The Mr. Varley, be it remarked, who is thus credited with "diluted insanity"—whatever that may mean—because he believed the evidence of his own senses against what Common Sense told him ought to be true, was none other than Mr. Cromwell Fleetwood Varley, F.R.S., C.E., who for many years was chief engineer to the Electric and International Telegraph Company, and who, in conjunction with his cousin, Michael Faraday, just quoted, discovered and demonstrated the laws governing the transmission of electricity through deep sea cables—an authority, therefore, presumably as respectable as Dr. Carpenter himself on scientific matters.

But, in fact, Dr. Carpenter, like so many other iconoclasts, was better than his creed. In the very next paragraph to that in which he credits his scientific confrère with "diluted insanity," he hedges thus:—

"At the same time, every one who admits that 'there are more things in heaven and earth than are dreamt of in our philosophy,' will be wise in maintaining 'a reserve of possibility' as to phenomena which are not altogether *opposed* to the Laws of Physics, but rather transcend them. Some of the writer's own experiences have led him to suspect that a power of intuitively perceiving what is passing in the mind of another, which has been designated as 'thought-reading,' may, like certain forms of sense-perception, be extraordinarily exalted by that entire concentration of the attention which is characteristic of the status we have been considering. There can be no question that this divining power is naturally possessed in a very remarkable degree by certain individuals, and that it may be greatly improved by cultivation. . . . Looking at nerve-force as a special form of physical energy, it may be deemed not altogether incredible that it should exert itself from a distance, so as to bring the brain of one person into direct dynamical communication with that of another, without the intermediation either of verbal language or of movements of expression. A large amount of evidence, sifted with the utmost care, would be needed to establish even a *probability* of such communication. But would any man of science have a right to say that it is *impossible?*"

Of course, in my *then* frame of mind, all these scientific dogmas appeared to me as undiluted priestcraft on the side of negation.

If we were to subjugate all our senses to the sovereignty of a mysterious something called "Common Sense" and spelt with capital letters, and if no amount of evidence was to outweigh the antecedent probabilities set down as the dicta of this sovereign "Common Sense," where were we? All belief was at an end, and we must receive as axioms anything which these "Men of Science"—still spelt with uncial initials—declared to be sober truth, and not "diluted insanity."

CHAPTER III

IN STATU PUPILLARI

"I merely mean to say what Johnson said,
　That in the course of some six thousand years,
All nations have believed that from the dead
　A visitant at intervals appears;
And what is strangest upon this strange head
　Is that whatever bar the reason rears
'Gainst such belief, there's something stronger still
In its behalf, let those deny who will."
　　　　　　　　　　　　　　　—BYRON.

IT may not unreasonably be asked how it happened that, if, as I supposed, I had found the pearl of great price, I did not straightway sell all I had and buy it? If I was really converted to belief in the Modern Mystery, why had I not the courage of my opinions? Why was I not prepared to accept, and to act out in a practical way, that which claimed to be a supplementary book of revelation, calculated to "make men believe in God"?

By way of reply to a question which I feel is—or was—by no means out of place, I would say, first of all, because I was "a pale-faced curate." I had, I think, settled it to my own satisfaction that there were the regularly ordained channels through which man might seek communion with the unseen, and he must use those channels or none. Beyond these it was not meant that he should go. He had no right to reckon on special providences. My wife, who had been so far *my* channel of communication, *my* special providence, holds the same opinion still. Her religious belief, however, has been all along so utterly unshadowed by doubt that she is perhaps on that account incapable of realising the case of persons not so steadfast in the faith. I had seen, and was destined afterwards to see, many instances where some such external buttress was absolutely necessary, and, to all appearance, operative for good.

But still I displayed none of the proverbial

enthusiasm of the newly converted. When we came back to England in the late summer of 1857, and made our home in the western suburbs of London, I continued my old work of pupilising and clerical duty, developing, after a time, into that of a regular schoolmaster; and only recurred to my new faith spasmodically at intervals few and far between.

One of my pupils was a young student who ultimately, after brilliant success at college and the bar, became Solicitor-General —I dare not, I suppose, say under what Government—and he has since laughingly alluded to the way in which we used to blend discussions of the Modern Mystery with our classical studies.

I very much wish I could mention this name; because I know how unsatisfactory initials, asterisks, and absence of personality are in such narratives as I have to give.

I shall perhaps seem to be violating my own self-imposed rule of silence when I add that another of my pupils was Ivanoff Autard de Bragard—now, I believe, a physician at Port Louis, Mauritius; but, in the first place, he is a long way off; and, in the second, his connection with the following story is so purely incidental that I scarcely think he could object to the casual mention of his name.

He was studying English with me, and at the same time preparing for his first communion at the hands of a Catholic priest in London. We varied our English studies, as the future Solicitor-General did his classical ones, by occasional deviations into the regions of the occult.

One day my wife wrote automatically some moral maxims, the exact purport of which I have forgotten; and it was stated that they came from a certain Louis Dupont, whose name was quite unknown to us all. When the lad paid his next visit to his priest, he was astounded to hear that ecclesiastic quote certain maxims from one Louis Dupont, deceased; and he showed his astonishment so plainly that the priest inquired the cause, and the youth told him what had taken place. He was, of course, forbidden to engage in any such pursuits for the future; but the incident made a great impression on him, as it did on all of us, because it seemed too difficult to cover the facts by any of the theories with which we were so far acquainted.

Another pupil, the brother of one of my young lady students in Paris, to whom I alluded above, also tried the experiment of asking mental questions, and answers were also given to these in automatic writing. After others of minor importance, the particulars of which I have forgotten, he said he had thought of one to which he should particularly like a reply. The sentence written down was the following bilingual one :—

"Ta mère est Catholique. Respect her faith."

The young man was almost as dumfoundered as I myself had been with my first experiences. His father was a Protestant, and his mother a Catholic; and he had mentally asked which was the true religion, the Catholic or the Protestant. He had lived so much abroad that he thought in French quite as much as in English; whilst I feel sure that the writer, if she had been elaborating the answer from her own inner consciousness, and inclined to adopt that hybrid expression of it, would have written "Votre mère," not "Ta mère."

It must not be supposed that these replies were so uniformly successful as in the cases quoted. One has continually to be on guard, not only in reading other people's stories, but in telling one's own, against the idea that everything is rose-coloured in such exceptional experiences as those which are now being recorded. Interspersed with these clear and lucid communications was any amount of nonsense and utter triviality. The net result of this admixture, supposing the transcendental theory to be accepted, would go far to prove that anything like rationality or common sense is almost more exceptional in the "spheres" than here below. Even ordinary truthfulness was by no means so universal as might have been desired. For example, the Road Murder was a topic of conversation about the time when the bilingual message just quoted was given; and naturally something was asked about the perpetrator of the crime. Instead of adhering to their frequently repeated principle that it was not the office of the communicating intelligence to name the guilty and ensure their punishment—"in which case earth would be what it was never meant to be, a perfect sphere"—they gave oracularly a long reply, in which they named the criminal, and added that one day, under a hedge, would be found the proofs of that person's guilt. Of course we could not check the statement then, and the circumstance of its being made in answer to a mental question was sufficiently curious to arrest attention; but subsequent discoveries proved that every detail of the communication was utterly and absolutely false.

"Nonum prematur in annum" was the practical advice given by Horace for properly maturing a literary composition; and I devoted a space of nine full years to the digestion of the new principles acquired at my "conversion" in 1856. I do not mean to say I gave all that long time to the thinking out of that one subject. There, I venture to suggest, is where persons who take up the study of occultism so frequently make a mistake They devote themselves exclusively to it, and so become people of one idea, or lose their heads altogether.

It would be an impertinence were I to dwell upon details of my own personal history, save in so far as they bear on the subject I have in hand. Suffice it to say, these nine years were very busy ones, during which I built up a large private school, and a numerous family gathered round me. But I never lost sight of my occultism. I held it, as it were, in reserve; and if any proof were necessary to show how serious a matter I deemed it, such would be afforded by the fact that I resolved, if ever I lost any one in whom I felt special interest, I would put my tenets to the proof by trying to establish communications with that one in the unseen world.

There I felt—and I feel it in a measure still—is the missing link which this supplementary revelation *might* supply. The fullest faith is conscious of an awful blank which meets us here "at our utmost need." What is it which happens in the process we call death? To soften down that expression, and call it "dissolution," "departure," or "passing away," is of no practical advantage. Whither does the freed spirit pass; to what does it depart? These are the fundamental questions on which the mind must fix itself when we contemplate either our own death, or that of the few who stand to us in the relation of second selves. In response to this natural demand we are met with an ominous silence in our churches and creeds. Had that silence been broken?

Acting on the hypothesis that it had, I thus registered a vow to test the supposition in case of such a contingency occurring to myself.

Little did I dream how soon that contingency was to occur!

This long period of nine years I have elected to call my state of pupillage. I was brooding over my new knowledge, holding it, as I said, in reserve, ready to be utilised when the necessity occurred. I had been fairly fortunate in my speculation. My school had developed beyond my most sanguine expectations, and my own boys were among my pupils; when suddenly, in the autumn of 1865, scarlet fever broke out. Several boys died, and among them my own little boy, Johnny, who had only just begun to attend the junior class, which was taught by a governess. I am obliged to give these details in consideration of what is to follow.

The child died under peculiarly painful circumstances. I had been compelled to send the patients away with the governess to a cottage in the suburbs, and he died before his mother and myself could reach him. All that happened thirty years ago, but it is printed on my memory like a picture. I can see now my wife coming into the schoolroom with the fatal telegram in her hand, summoning me from my class to the boy's deathbed. I can remember every stage of the journey on that sombre morning of late October, which seemed as if it were prophetic of the result. Then we got to our little homestead, and found the Dark Shadow had crossed its threshold before us. All those years have passed, yet the pathos of that event has never passed away or diminished from me. It was my "first great sorrow." The child was, in some sort, a favourite with me, and just at an age when a boy begins to be a companion. He was snatched away from me with awful suddenness, and my previous exemption from sorrow made me break down more completely than I might otherwise have done under the blow. I forget where I read the following lines—which I quote from memory—but they expressed my own feelings at this time so exactly that they have haunted me ever since :—

> " Then gently did he usher us within
> The Holy of Holies of a father's heart,
> Where sat the first great sorrow, still and stern,
> The dark, unfeatured guest, now fading slow
> In hallowed, healing light."

Will the most "critical" reader question my seriousness when I state that, with that little coffin open before us, where lay the bright boy who would never again join our broken home-circle, his mother and myself sat down to ask the meaning of this strange visitation?

She took pencil in hand; and of course it will be supposed that she received a little loving message from the child she had lost. *Such was not the case.* A message was written, not purporting to emanate from the child, but from a Guardian Spirit to whose tutelage he had passed, and who gave the name of "The Anointed." That spirit was —so he claimed—of a different order from those who generally communicate with persons on the material plane. The child formed the connecting link between himself and the mother, rendering possible an intercourse which, it was added, was specially designed for *my* edification.

Will the supposed critic even call my judgment in question when I say that I accepted heartily—in the most literal sense of that last word—the comforting doctrine thus given to us? What was it, after all, but an adaptation to my own necessities of that doctrine about Guardian Angels which I had always held, though it constitutes no clause in the Church's formal creed. Said not the Master Himself that in heaven the angels of the little children always behold the Father's face?

Gerald Massey had passed through the same twofold ordeal as ourselves when he wrote:—

"O ye who say, 'We have a child in heaven,'
And know how far away that heaven may seem;
Who have felt the desolate isolation sharp
Defined in Death's own face; who have stood beside
The Silent River, and stretched out pleading hands
For some sweet babe upon the other bank,
That went forth where no human hand might lead,
And left the shut house with no light, no sound,
No answer when the mourners wail without!
What we have known ye know—ye only know."

At all events, I resolved that, so far as possible, here my state of pupillage should end. I would, if so it might be, seek initiation into the mysteries. Let the hardheaded people smile if they will, I believe my new revelation, as I deemed it, did steady me when I felt ready to reel under an unaccustomed blow.

It left room for hope—hope at a time when we are mostly hopeless. How far that hope was well grounded it is my object in recording these experiences to show.

CHAPTER IV

THE HYPNOTIC BORDERLAND

> "Sleep, sleep on! forget thy pain,
>   My hand is on thy brow,
> My spirit on thy brain,
> My pity on thy heart, poor friend;
> And from my fingers flow
>   The powers of life, and, like a sign
> Seal thee from thine hour of woe,
>   And brood on thee, but may not blend with thine.
> .   .   .   .
> Sleep, sleep, and with the slumber of
>   The dead and the unborn
> Forget thy life and love:
> Forget that thou must wake; for ever
>   Forget the world's dull scorn;
> Forget lost health. . . ."   —SHELLEY.

> "A great perturbation in nature! to receive at once the benefit of sleep, and do the effects of watching. In this slumbery agitation, besides her walking and other actual performances, what, at any time, have you heard her say?"
> —SHAKESPEARE.

So far I have dealt with what I would, under due protest, call the most vulgar phases of that multifarious subject comprehensively termed the Modern Mystery. Tilts, raps and automatic writing were the forms in which communications were most commonly made while the wave of occultism was at first cresting; and in no other sense do I use the possibly objectionable epithet, though some even of the initiates themselves hold that these manifestations are the most "material" methods employed for the conveyance of messages from "the other side." The more subjective phenomena stand higher in their esteem; though these, they still argue, would probably be less effective for establishing a nascent faith, because they are less readily checked by sight and sense than the objective, physical manifestations. The agents are, as it were, "acting to the gallery" when they spin tables, knock furniture about, and write crude messages in a schoolboy hand.

Our experience of the raps had not been nearly so copious as with the tilts and, in even a greater degree, the writing, though the first-mentioned form of communication was sometimes adopted. First would come a faint tap on the table exactly like the pecking of a bird. This would be followed by louder raps resembling the tap of a finger not so much on as *in* the table. The noise, that is, could not be localised above or below the surface, but seemed to proceed rather from the interior. It is difficult to describe this peculiarity to one who has never realised it by experience. On several occasions I have heard the rap so loud that it seemed to be produced by a smart slap of the open hand. This was particularly the case, I remember, when a well-known pianist was performing. The bangs were so loud as apparently to endanger the safety of the grand piano-case on which they were administered. This, I should add, was in the darkness, when the manifestations were generally more violent; but most of our domestic séances, and all of those where writing was used, took place in full light.

But now, once again in the most unexpected way, I was to have an experience of what I would call the subjective phase of occultism.

The governess who presided over my junior school, had attended our little boy in his last illness, and had herself taken the fever. Hers was a very severe case, while it left her with her right arm fixed rigidly to her side, and quite useless. Of course this was a very serious matter for her, and I felt a certain amount of responsibility, as she had presumably taken the fever from my child.

I had been reading the Rev. Chauncy Hare Townshend's work, "Facts in Mesmerism," and especially his strange experiences with the celebrated somnambulist, Alexis Didier, in Paris. The book appeared to me very fairly written, and the value of Mr. Townshend's testimony was enhanced to me by the fact that Charles Dickens wrote a laudatory introduction to the collection of his "Religious Opinions," acting as literary executor to his friend.

Now it occurred to me that mesmerism, as it was then called—for the later and more satisfactory title of hypnotism was so far unknown—might be advantageously used in the case of this governess. A brother of Alexis, M. Didier, was practising as a medical magnetist in Kensington, and I felt I should like him to try his hand—literally so—on the case.

One day I came home somewhat late in the evening, and found my wife and the governess installed in my study. The latter was ensconced in an easy-chair, actively doing nothing — an occupation, let me remark, for which she had a special faculty; and this peculiarity is of great importance for the part she was destined to play in my occult studies.

"Why, you look exactly as if you were going to be magnetised," I said, having in my mind the picture of Alexis in the "sleep-waking" condition. "Shall I try my skill upon you?"

She consented, and I forthwith set to work, carrying out as closely as I was able the directions given in Townshend's book. In twenty minutes she was sound asleep; but this was no unusual experience with the lady in question, who was as prone to "drop off" as the fat boy in "Pickwick" himself. I felt I must have some test to assure myself that this was a case of "magnetic" sleep, and not an instance of tired nature's sweet restorer.

Now, I knew if the slumber was of the magnetic kind, the sleeper would be able to respond to my inarticulate thoughts — to answer a mental question, that is, in the language of my previous experiences.

I put a question, therefore, in that way— simply *thinking it*, and not articulating the demand. She answered readily, and we kept up an animated conversation, much to my wife's amusement and mystification, as she could only hear the answers, not the questions.

For very obvious reasons, I made it a rule, without any exception whatsoever, that I would never exercise this power save in presence of a third person; and under the circumstances now being detailed, that third person was naturally my wife. I take this opportunity of warning all investigators into the phenomena of animal magnetism, not to neglect such a necessary precaution.

Having thus satisfactorily made the double discovery that I was a magnetist, and that I had a receptive subject under my own roof, I went at a bound into this different, but by no means disconnected, domain of occult study.

The first thing I did was to arrange with M. Didier for half-a-dozen practical lessons in the manipulation of magnetic subjects. He gave me two of these lessons, and then abruptly refused to continue his instruction. I asked him why; and he said—

"Because you do not need teaching. You

magnetise instinctively. Why do you put your thumbs in the particular position you do when you magnetise me?"

I had certainly sent him to sleep very easily; but I accounted for this by his sensitiveness. I had no notion why I disposed of my thumbs in that particular fashion; and I told him so.

"Precisely; because you are a born magnetist. And let me add," he continued, "from what you tell me of your subject, she is one in a thousand."

From this time forth, for some long while, our studies took a magnetic turn, and the table was quite put on one side; though my wife still wrote, and got some very strange communications from the Anointed on that, to us, engrossing topic, the condition of children in the world beyond.

It will perhaps disappoint my readers when I tell them I trifled with this new phase of the subject; but I am going to be as candid, at all events, in these "Confessions" as Jean Jacques Rousseau himself.

Beyond the initial discovery that "our life is twofold," and that the magnetic life is cut off absolutely from ordinary waking existence, I found out this—that any promise made in the magnetic state would be faithfully carried out in common life, though the subject had no notion that she was acting under compulsion of any kind. This, of course, opened up a wide and too tempting field for experimentation. I was young then, and could not resist.

They were the days of large crinolines; and my subject was of Amazonian proportions. Suddenly she paraded the streets with garments as scanty and straight as those of a Grecian heroine. The little boys laughed, and her friends remonstrated; but she said the prevailing fashion was ugly and ridiculous, and she would never conform to it again. She was quite indignant when I said she would return to her former garb on the following Thursday. Having got over the difficulty of discarding it, she was not likely, she said, to resume it. But she did resume it on the Thursday, since I had, in the meantime, exacted a promise to that effect in the magnetic condition. She varied her diet even more frequently than her dress. She had a good healthy appetite, with marked proclivities for certain viands; but to these she now showed the strongest aversion. She had made a mesmeric promise not to touch them.

All this—and more that I could tell—seems trivial enough; but, when one comes to think of it, how strangely it bears on the subject of *motives!*

There was, however, a more distinctly marked borderland between this hypnotic condition and the occult phenomena technically so termed. One night when she had been hypnotised as usual, and was walking about my study in obedience to my command, I noticed that the pupils of her eyes were moving under the closed lids. I asked her how this was, and she said, "For the first time, I see light."

I knew what this meant; and it was well I did, and was prepared for the result. She was passing into the state of lucidity, which is looked upon as a higher condition than clairvoyance. She could get to the light, she said, if I would *let* her, and would magnetise her more deeply. She told me how to do this; and when I had succeeded, she threw herself on the sofa, and looked precisely like a dead person. That indescribable refinement came over her features which we see in the dead. She was utterly oblivious of all persons living, but said she knew she was close to the departed. I mentioned my wife's name, which happened to be the same as that of her deceased mother. "Oh yes, you mean mamma," she said. "Yes, if you will let me, I can go to her." She knew the name of my dead child, but had forgotten the living one, who was her special favourite.

Truly this seemed a veritable borderland, a link between the worlds seen and unseen!

I spoke just now of the constant presence of my wife at these "magnetic" séances; but she did her best to negative the value of her presence on this occasion by retiring to the stairs and going into hysterics, being alarmed at the corpse-like appearance of my "subject" and the gruesome nature of the conversation in which we were engaged. I thus had two patients on my hands for a short period; but the hysterics soon passed away, and I had nothing to do but to recall my sleeper from the land of dreams—if, indeed, it was to the realm of shadows rather than of realities to which she had passed.

When I proceeded to demesmerise her, she protested strongly. She did not want to "come back," she said. I told her if she did not come back she would die; to which she made answer, "I *want* to die."

When I questioned her as to the light she

was so anxious to reach, she said, "I think it comes from God;" and then, as if correcting herself, she added, "I think it *is* God."

I myself was so awe-stricken with the solemnity of this phase that I did not often repeat it. I dreaded to think what might have been the result had I lost my nerve; but, as I said, I was prepared for the result, and therefore not surprised.

She herself has never known anything of what took place on these occasions, but will read the account for the first time in these pages.

A physician who saw this case in all its phases often advised me to publish its details; but I have never done so in full.

My wife had a serious illness at this time, and was attended by the medical man in question, who told me to mesmerise the governess and let her diagnose the disease. I did so; and though she was fairly reticent as a rule, she posed at once as a medical man, took her place by the bedside, and said to me,

"Do you not see what is amiss?"—she supposed I could see what was clairvoyantly visible to herself—"Can you not perceive, therefore, that she is being wrongly treated?"

The physician adopted implicitly the view taken by the clairvoyant; though, for our mutual satisfaction, he called in for consultation a second physician, who was a specialist in such cases, and who exactly confirmed the diagnosis of the governess. It was decided that the medicines then being administered should be discontinued, and that the cure should be intrusted solely to magnetisation. As a matter of fact it was so performed, and the patient is a living witness to its efficacy.

Here, then, was another and most interesting phase of this Protean subject. Among the Pentecostal charisms of the Church whereof I was an ordained minister, this gift of healing by the laying on of hands stood pre-eminent. It had lain dormant for centuries; what if it were being revived?

I had been entirely successful in restoring the paralysed arm of the governess. In her waking state it was pinned closely to her side. Say this was due to hysteria, and that there was no organic mischief, as I think most probably the case; the fact remained. Whereas her arm had been useless, it was now restored, whole as the other. She had ceased attempting to use it, and kept it, as I said, pinned to her side. Directly I magnetised her I made her assume the attitude of the eagle-slayer; the result being that after a few treatments the cure was radically, and, as events proved, permanently effected.

My wife's sister too had for years suffered from a paralysed arm, and I took her to Didier for advice. I threw him into the magnetic sleep; and, in that condition, he gave a complete history of the case, which I myself did not know, and prescribed my magnetisation as the remedy. I began to operate, and had the satisfaction of seeing tendon after tendon stirring, the patient assuring me that she now felt sensation in the withered arm for the first time during all those years. But the treatment was too exhausting for me, and I went to tell Didier that such was the case.

Directly I entered his consulting-room, he laughed and said, "I know what you have come for: you cannot go on with that case."

I told him he was right; and he explained, "Your patient is like a sponge; she absorbs the whole of the vitality from you." He was obliged, he said, to charge himself by means of a medical battery before he could undertake such a case.

But even these instances of healing, strange as they were, sank into insignificance in my estimation, compared with the importance of the link between mesmerism and those other manifestations which had preceded it in my experience. The order is usually inverted; mesmerism for the most part leads the neophyte up to the vestibule of the temple, where the deeper mysteries are to meet him. In my case years elapsed before mesmerism came in to give, as it were, the key of the portal.

I was now pledged to initiation, and resolved to place myself without delay in the hands of the hierophant. I had reached that point where it was difficult to draw back, and where there was every inducement to advance —such inducement resolving itself into the effort to prove unbroken continuity between the life in this world and the life beyond.

While these pages were being written, there appeared an article on hypnotism in the columns of the *Westminster Gazette*. Having just boomed its "exposure" of the Mahatmas, that journal proceeded to demolish hypnotism so far as it claimed to be a branch of the occult. I know not who wrote the article in question, but he wielded a very different pen to that which was used by Mr. Garrett in his brilliant crusade against the "masters" and their adherents.

"It is, of course, true that many of the problems which encounter one in the study of hypnotism are still unsolved, and thus are open to the imaginative writer to deal with almost as he pleases. No one can object to that; indeed, it is possible that science may learn something by his flights of fancy. But he cannot go against the commonplaces of hypnotic knowledge. It will interest many, and dispel not a few bogeys, to enumerate these briefly.

"(a) The hypnotist cannot suddenly by any tricks with his hands and eyes send any person into a trance. In nineteen cases out of twenty, to produce hypnosis even gradually is a task that occupies two hours a day for several days together. It may take almost a month, *even when the patient is doing everything in his power to assist the operator*.

"(b) No one can, in the first instance, be hypnotised against his will. The only exception to this is the very rare case where, by the application of gentle heat in a peculiar cap-shaped vessel to the patient's head, hypnosis can be induced in sleep. This is sometimes tried in difficult cases, but even then failure is more likely than not.

"(c) All control is purely the result of suggestion, aural or otherwise. There is not the slightest ground for believing that telepathic influence can be exerted; and where this is apparently done, it is the result of previous suggestion, or of a suggestion not noticed by the witnesses.

"(d) From this it follows that the hypnotic 'power,' or 'influence,' or 'willing,' is nothing more than applied knowledge; and it follows, again, that any ordinary intelligent person can to some extent learn how to use this knowledge.

"(e) The dangers of hypnotism are, as a rule, physical, *i.e.*, it is difficult to know whether clonic or tonic convulsions may not come on, and any ignorant experimenter may kill the patient.

"(f) The possibility of a hypnotiser using

his knowledge for nefarious purposes can be avoided by insisting that the first suggestion made shall be that the patient shall not do or consent to anything which he would not do or permit in his normal state. This 'previous limiting suggestion' is usually, or, at any rate, frequently, employed by therapeutists.

"(g) The hypnotic control, even when thoroughly established, *tends invariably to die out of itself*, and in ordinary cases no suggestion will be valid for more, let us say, than three months, unless it is repeated.

"From this it is easy to see that the assumptions of the fiction-writer are based on an entire misconception of the theory of hypnotism. The notion, for instance, that the operator is unable to release his victim from his 'spell' is too ludicrous for words. For there is no magic 'spell' to begin with, and any control he may have obtained can be done away with by suggestion, just as it was obtained by suggestion. To such an extent is this true that the hypnotist can, by a strong suggestion to that effect, prevent his throwing his own patient into the hypnotic state for any given time.

"The 'will' of the operator has in no case anything to do with the matter, and all the dramatic scenes we read in which the mind of the man with this 'power' sways the mind of his victim or instrument are as baseless as they are absurd and harmful. For hypnotism, properly used by authorised practitioners, is full of promise as a curative agent, and both public stage performers and writers who foster false notions on the subject are reprehensible."

Many of the positions here laid down I should, as in some sense a practical hypnotist, be inclined to traverse. With regard to the prolixity of the process, according to this anonymous authority, my own experience as already detailed is quite at variance; and I have another incident which seems to prove that the will is the agent, and that it exerts what the Psychical Research Society have taught us to call a "telepathic" influence, quite independently of any overt act on the operator's part.

As a relief from the monotony of schoolwork, I used to have a musical meeting in my schoolroom every Friday evening, when the week's work was practically over. On one of these occasions, as I was passing through the drawing-room where my guests were assembled, I overheard the principal vocalist of the evening say that she had once been mesmerised. It was, I suppose, little more than the spirit of mischief which prompted me to resolve that I would then and there try my skill upon her. I sat down in a corner of the crowded room, took a book, opened it at a blank page and pretended to be reading. I was, however, intensely *willing* that this lady should be mesmerised. I made no sign, I never removed my eyes from the blank page, and in a very short space of time —it was impossible I should be long undisturbed—that lady rose abruptly, made a rush for the bedroom, and told my wife, who had followed her in alarm, that she was obliged to go, because I was mesmerising her, and she should have "gone off" if she had stayed longer.

I trust I shall not be deemed over-scrupulous if I here repeat my warning against the indiscriminate use of this power, or if I urge the need of witnesses. With all due respect to the writer in the *Westminster Gazette*, I know that the power of the magnetiser's will is practically unlimited, and therefore the possibilities of malpractice or the slightest loophole for suspicion cannot be too jealously guarded against.

It is now many years since I have attempted to exercise this power; but in place of the operator I have become the patient, and can bear unqualified testimony to the value of hypnotism as a curative agent. I suffer from periodical attacks of a painful disease in the eyes, which my medical advisers frankly confessed baffled them. They could only prescribe strict regimen as a means of making the visitations less frequent. One Sunday quite recently I was officiating alone in a West End church, and had been troubled a good deal during the service and sermon. A lady came into the vestry at the conclusion and said she could cure me, proffering her services gratuitously. I knew something of her as a masseuse, and, of course, thanked her; but so many specifics had been offered me by different people that I thought little of this last suggestion, until a member of the congregation, who had witnessed this lady's success in similar cases, advised me to let her try. I did so, and she was completely successful, removing the obstruction which medical men had failed to reach. After doing this, she suggested that my brain was much overworked, and that a short hypnotic sleep would be a relief to me. She was surprised to find that I was quite willing to be operated upon; and after a few passes I felt myself nod. I lifted my head again, instantaneously as I thought, but was surprised to find myself alone, and to learn by the timepiece on the mantelshelf that I had been oblivious for twenty-five minutes. The relief was marvellous; and I never afterwards omitted to solicit a renewal of this refreshment when the purely medical treatment was over. My medical man was staggered when he heard of its success, declaring that, on every statement of the facts—which I dare say he received *cum grano*—the whole thing was simply miraculous.

I often wished to test the duration of the hypnotic influence by letting my own patient remain until she awoke of her own accord without being demesmerised; but there were practical difficulties in the way of this experiment. My subject had frequently said I could only exert my power over her when close at hand. One part of my clerical duties at that time consisted in taking a short service to some troops from nine to ten on Sunday morning. I said to her therefore, "If I send you to sleep next Sunday morning at half-past nine, you will know I must be mesmerising you at the distance of a mile at least." She assented, but added that, of course, as I had forewarned her, she would be on her guard, and take care to keep particularly wide awake. I only added, "Next Sunday morning you will go to sleep at 9.30 and wake at 10." At 9.30 she was talking to my wife, when she suddenly rose and tried to get to her bedroom, but only succeeded in getting as far as the boys' dormitory, where she threw herself on a bed and sank into profound slumber. My wife, alarmed lest the boys and servants should discover the hanky-panky that was being practised, at last bethought her of a device. She shook the sleeper and said, "It is ten o'clock now," rather anticipating the order of events; but it was quite sufficient. My patient rose, and never afterwards questioned my telepathic powers. That the influence of the operator's will was paramount, I proved in this case; and I cannot help thinking this fact must be taken into consideration when the claims of hypnotism as a curative agent are being asserted.

Of course, with the lapse of years, all the influence has long since passed away, since it has never been renewed. This lady and myself still meet as ordinary acquaintances, and as though we had never set foot together across the mysterious frontier-line of the hypnotic borderland.

Fortunately, as Père Lacordaire said, "Le somnambule parait savoir des choses qu'il ignorait avant son sommeil, et"—this is to my present point—"qu'il oublie à l'instant du réveil."

One conversation with my regular "subject" I must report, even at the risk of disturbing her truly eligible oblivion; for I believe she has never been made aware until now of the part she took in it.

After one of the musical evenings mentioned above, we were supping together, and amongst our guests was the conductor of our little band, a violinist of no mean celebrity, Herr Otto von Booth, who at that time manifested a thoroughly Teutonic incredulity in respect of all my marvellous stories; but I believe he has changed front since, much as I did myself, though I do not quite know his position, physical or psychological, at present. He seemed quite unable to associate any transcendental ideas with that far from ethereal governess.

"Very well," I said. "The next time you sup with us, mention the word 'Mendelssohn' casually, and then refer to the violin as a perfect instrument; I shall be surprised if you do not hear some new views enunciated."

He mentioned Mendelssohn; and that governess, not usually pragmatic, but previously prepared by me, though unconscious of such preparation, literally flew at our innocent conductor. Mendelssohn she held to be an utterly overrated man. His compositions were beneath contempt; the dance music of Dan Godfrey ranking far higher as works of art. Then as to the violin being a perfect instrument, that idea she held to be equally mythical. The large brass instrument played by a certain boy in the band, and technically known as the bombardon, was infinitely superior in intonation. Never shall I forget that artist's face, or, for the matter of that, the expression of the speaker, who felt she had been advancing somewhat revolutionary opinions.

I must leave my subject—in more senses than one—here, though I could expatiate at far greater length. I once contributed a short paper to a very widely circulated periodical giving a résumé of this case; and I was perfectly inundated with letters, many of them from medical men, asking for fuller particulars. I have, however, said perhaps as much as is necessary, and feel no necessity to multiply words. Indeed, it is more than probable that, although hypnotism is now accepted as a scientific fact, its clear connection with occultism, as shown in the above narrative, will be a novel feature to many readers, and possibly overtax the receptive powers of not a few.

CHAPTER V

IN THE HANDS OF THE MASTERS

"Most potent, grave, and reverend signiors,
My very noble and approved good masters."
—SHAKESPEARE.

AT the time of which I write, the foremost man in the Modern Mystery—I had nearly written "the leading spirit," but that might give a false impression—was Mr. Benjamin Coleman, who was in personal appearance and general character about the last one would ever have suspected of having anything to do with transcendentalism. He was a hard-headed, outspoken man of business, and how he became converted to the new doctrines I never heard; but he was wholly committed to them, and readily took me in hand when I wrote to him recounting my experiences and intimating a desire to know more. He was, I believe, both proprietor and editor of *The Spiritual Magazine*, the proprietorship consisting in paying the expenses of production, and the editorship being equally a labour of love. I doubt whether the literary phase of this movement has ever been a very remunerative one. I afterwards wrote a good deal in the pages of this magazine, but always gratuitously; indeed, with the exception of occasional leading articles in the earlier numbers of *Light*, which is still a flourishing organ of this body, I do not think I ever pursued my calling as a professional journalist in connection with the movement.

I am writing from memory the events of thirty years ago, and may be pardoned if I am not always strictly chronological in the order of my incidents. I mention this matter because I want to set down a curious occurrence which belongs to a very early part of my acquaintance with Mr. Coleman, and it is possible that, without some such previous explanation, I might be called to order as to my dates.

Mr. Coleman lived near the Crystal Palace, and I received an invitation from him to attend a meeting in one of the rooms of that building and witness the doings of two remarkable personages with whom he had met somewhere in the provinces. They claimed only to be conjurers; but Mr. Coleman assured me they were "mediums" without knowing it, or, at all events, without confessing it. They were the now celebrated Messrs. Maskelyne and Cook, the most ruthless exposers of the Modern Mystery in existence. I believe the theory held by most of the transcendental people who attended those meetings—for two were held—was that Mr. Cook was the medium, and that Mr. Maskelyne filled up any defects with prestidigitation; but Mr. Coleman would not hear a word about conjuring. They were both mediums, whether they chose to acknowledge it or not; and when Mr. Coleman made up his mind on any point, it was not worth while to contradict him. I do not know what he said—though I can guess—when Messrs. Maskelyne and Cook soon after assumed the unique position which they have maintained to the present day. He has been dead some years, as indeed have all the "masters" of whom I shall have to speak in the present chapter.

Several years after, when Mr. Maskelyne had made the "exposure" of so-called spiritualism his speciality, a certain Dr. Sexton undertook the utterly gratuitous task of "exposing" Mr. Maskelyne. He did, for a fact, show how some of his mechanical tricks were accomplished, such as getting out of a corded box; but the learned doctor, who was a shrewd, sensible man in his way, failed to see, or chose to ignore, the false logic of "exposing" one who, from first to last, protested against being set down as a medium, even *malgré lui*.

The very first step which Mr. Coleman took when I placed myself as a neophyte in his hierophantic hands was to carry me off triumphantly to the Beethoven Rooms, Harley Street, where I was to hear a wonderful " inspirational speaker "—Miss Emma Hardinge. I did not recognise the name at first, though it seemed to have a familiar sound.

Directly I entered the room, however, and found myself face to face with the occupant of the platform, I turned in some surprise and said to my cicerone, " I know that lady.'

Instead of being pleased, as I had expected, Mr. Coleman seemed annoyed, and begged me not to mention my previous acquaintance above my breath. Where had I known Miss Emma Hardinge, and when?

"In the year 1850," I replied. "She was an actress at the Adelphi Theatre."

He nodded assent, and repeated his request that I would not publish the fact.

"But," I rejoined, "if that lady proves a speaker at all, it will be the most amazing testimony as to the influence brought to bear upon her."

It was throwing words away. Those histrionic antecedents were—most unwisely, as I thought, and still think—to be rigidly suppressed.

The fact was that, sixteen years before, Miss Emma Hardinge, then a very young actress, was playing at the Adelphi with Wright, Paul Bedford, Mrs. Frank Matthews, and other veterans in the profession, who delighted to "gag," and often threw this young lady into utter confusion, for she could not depart one iota from her lines. I remembered one farce in particular in which this "gagging" took place; and we youths delighted to go to the pit night after night to see poor Emma Hardinge bewildered by the liberties her seniors took with the text of the dramatist; but now I was to accept her as an inspirational speaker, who would discourse on any subject, however recondite, that might be proposed by the audience after she had taken her place on the platform and got "under control" as it was called.

What the afflatus was, if not what it claimed to be, inspiration from without, I could not guess; but I recollect to this hour my amazement when I heard long fluent discourses on such subjects as "Hades" and "Mystery" delivered without a moment's pause or hesitation, and of necessity impromptu, by one whom I had known previously only as being utterly dumfoundered by the slightest deviation from the *litera scripta* of an Adelphi farce!

It so happened that whilst I was thus "sitting under" my inspirational speaker, I met Mrs. Frank Matthews and related my experiences to her.

"What?" she exclaimed, "Emma Hardinge an inspirationist? I never knew a girl so utterly destitute of the power to put ten words together!"

Therein, I repeat, lay the marvel for me. But these good transcendental folks were too thin-skinned to let me bear my testimony. I hope I am not giving offence to anybody by putting it forward after this long lapse of years.

Of course, even these fluent discourses lost their attractive power after a time, so far as I was concerned. Not so with the elect. Their patience is phenomenal. They will go on witnessing exactly the same "manifestations." I was just as much puzzled as ever, but one cannot go on being puzzled indefinitely without getting a little wearied of the sensation.

Dr. Donovan, who used at that time to run a Phrenological Institute in the Strand, was outspoken enough to put this doctrine into words one night. Addressing Mr. Coleman, who was presiding, he said, "Mr. Chairman, can't you give us a little variety? We are charmed with the speaker's powers; but, after all, it's not such an unusual thing to hear a lady talk fluently. We should like a change."

This dissentient auditor was promptly demolished, and the inspired speaker pursued the even tenor of her way.

It was at one of these inspirational speechifications, too, that I met another of my Masters, Mr. Frederick Hockley, who was certainly on the whole the most "all-round" occultist I have ever known. My meeting with him was purely accidental. I sat next him, and we got into conversation on the one absorbing topic. When I told him my wife was an automatic writer, he strongly advised me to discontinue that mode of communication. I asked him why; and he replied that it was simply "possession." The writer's organism was controlled by an external intelligence, and who, he asked, could guarantee what the character of that intelligence might be? The form of communication he adopted was that of crystal-seeing or looking into the consecrated mirror. There the vision was purely objective, and no danger need be apprehended.

He invited me to his rooms, which I found hung round with these mirrors, each being consecrated to some special "spirit." His principal informant was an intelligence calling himself "The Crowned Angel;" and he had volumes of communications received from that source. He had no power of sight himself, and had unfortunately lost his "speculatrix" some years before. She was the daughter of persons with whom he had lodged at Croydon, and her faculty was developed when she was only thirteen years of age. She had gone on exercising it until she was twenty, when she died. The communications were certainly far above what might have been expected from a person of her age and position, being apocalyptic in character, and often strangely confirmed as to matters of fact about which she could have no possible knowledge.

When Lieutenant, afterwards Sir Richard, Burton was about to set out on his expedition to Mecca, he applied to Mr. Hockley for a consecrated mirror, as being part of the paraphernalia of an Arab physician — the character he intended to assume. Having supplied him with this, Mr. Hockley asked if he might call him into his mirror during his journey. He received permission, and some long time afterwards made the invocation. The little girl described a scene where for a considerable period nothing but sand was visible. She pictured the travellers making their way across this, and among them was one whom Mr. Hockley identified as Burton. Then they came to a spot where there were trees and water, where they encamped and lighted their pipes. Presently another band of travellers came up, and there was a quarrel between the leader of this band and Burton. Their gestures were threatening, and by-and-by a little black boy came up, struck the pipe out of Burton's mouth, and so made peace. Years after, Major Burton confirmed all these particulars. At the very date when the child saw him, the incident occurred which formed the only peril he encountered in his journey. As Burton's caravan were encamped in an oasis, a party of Wahabee Arabs came up, and ordered them to put out their pipes, as they had conscientious scruples against tobacco. Burton, of course, refused, and high words passed, when his little negro seer, who was a privileged person, put an end to the strife by knocking Burton's pipe out of his mouth exactly as described by the girl at Croydon. I am telling the story from memory only, because I feel that in so doing I am adhering as closely as possible to my plan of a personal narrative; but since writing it, I have had the opportunity of referring to Mr. Hockley's MS., where I find the facts set down in the main as I remembered them from his own words. Eight years afterwards, Burton again called on Mr. Hockley, and wrote on the page opposite to that containing the narrative the following words :—

"*I quite recognise the correctness of this vision—the old grey man, the boy, and the quarrel about the pipe. This is easily ascertained by a reference to the '* Pilgrimage.'

"RICHARD F. BURTON."

Mr. Hockley lent me one of his crystals, and my wife saw a little in it; but, by his advice, I left it on the mantelpiece of my study. Somebody, he said, would be sure to see in it. The seer in my case proved to be a housemaid, who, on looking at the crystal, described it as becoming clouded and appearing as if filled with milk. This, we knew, was a sign that she would "see." Presently the milkiness cleared away, and the girl saw a series of visions, but nothing beyond the average housemaid intelligence. Here, however, was another phase of this multiform subject. The girl became so fascinated with the crystal that we were forced to put it out of sight.

Mr. Hockley had a large collection of books on occultism written in all languages, though he himself read nothing but English.

He was partner in a firm of chartered accountants in the City, and looked as little like an occultist—well, as Mr. Coleman himself. He tried to teach me astrology, but found me hopelessly unteachable; and moreover gave me certain "spells," though he strongly advised me never to use them, as they formed part of "black magic," which could not be practised without danger. I need scarcely say I did not heed his advice, but proved at once the efficacy of the spells, and their perils. Upon this branch of my subject, however, I must preserve comparative silence; for he refused to give me any information until I had solemnly promised, first, that I would not use the spells for any evil purpose, and secondly, that I would never communicate to any one the *modus operandi*.

So much as this I may say. His theory was that in using these spells we were working with low — rather, perhaps, than necessarily evil — spiritual agency. The mere formularies and manual acts employed were of no import beyond strengthening the will to enforce the co-operation of these intelligences; but for such co-operation we were always liable to have a *quid pro quo* exacted. I am simply setting down the rationale of these processes as expounded to me at that time by this particular Master.

I find myself placed in a somewhat awkward dilemma, between my desire to communicate to my readers as much as possible of this most curious department in all my complex subject, and the really stringent conditions under which the information was originally given to myself. Without speaking plainly—more plainly than is consistent with observance of my promise—I know I must fail to convey the actual terror which I feel, after all this space of time, when I contemplate my slender advance into the weird region of black magic. That terror is really almost as palpable now as it was when I made my first experiment.

I hesitated a long time before taking the plunge, and consulted the intelligence which was always at my wife's beck and call, without, however, saying what the project was which I had in my mind; but I was warned that absolute secrecy was necessary to success. Might I, I asked, carry out that project?

"Yes," was the reply; "to the pure all things are pure. Do it once only, just to convince yourself."

"Have you any further directions to give me," I inquired, "in addition to those I have received?"

"Yes; you must repeat the mystic words three times three."

Remember, the writer knew nothing of the project. I might have been dabbling in stocks or backing a horse.

The special experiment I chose was the forcing a person's presence. Of course, I chose a stranger to operate upon. It would have been no test had I selected a person who might have come to me under ordinary circumstances. It was a man who filled a somewhat prominent public position, whom I had seen once only, and with whom I had no acquaintance.

I had to rise in the middle of the night and go through certain rites which I scarcely think I would detail if I were at liberty to do so, and which I certainly would not repeat on any consideration now. More than this I must not say.

I waited anxiously during the following morning and afternoon to see whether the person in question would put in an appearance, and wondering what he would say if he did, since he could have no possible excuse for calling upon me.

As he did not come during the day, I concluded my experiment had failed, and at evening, though somewhat later than usual, I went, according to my custom, to read the papers. When I returned *there was the man's card on my study table.*

He had left no message, the servant said,

but simply thrust the card into her hand and made off, seeming, she thought, rather relieved than otherwise that I was not in. I took occasion to write to him at the large public institution where he was officially engaged, since his card bore no address. I said I had found his card on my return, and regretted that I had not been at home when he called, asking him kindly to state his business; but I received no reply.

I never traced any evil results from this experiment. Perhaps it was permissible under the circumstances named above, being the one experiment made for purposes of conviction. Afterwards it became a matter of mere idle curiosity; for, I am sorry to say, I did repeat the experiment then, and suffered in consequence. I cannot go into details, but it is no mere matter of opinion. The evil results were, beyond all controversy, directly attributable to the act, and to nothing else. It was physically impossible that the person operated upon could be present; any sort of communication was a matter of extreme difficulty; but the difficulties were overcome, and the catastrophe came.

I have since seen this spell in print, and could, if I so chose, give book, chapter, and verse to my readers; but such a course would be as palpable an evasion of my promise as though I set down full directions in my own pages.

Mr. Hockley, by the way, gave me an amusing illustration of one special danger attending lack of discretion in these matters. He himself had considerable proclivities for sporting pursuits in his younger days, though the combination with a taste for occultism seems somewhat grotesque. Occasionally he would prolong his stay at some town where races were being held, beyond the limits he had originally proposed. All of a sudden he would feel an uncontrollable desire to go home. Whatever the hour of night or day might be, he must set off at once. He felt sure his wife was working that spell, and afterwards found out that such was the case. I forget how she had got hold of it, whether from his books and MSS., or whether, Samson-like, he had told her in some moment of connubial confidence. What would not some of my female readers give for such a method of recalling their errant lords? It was only done by way of practical joke in this instance, for my friend was by no means erratic, nor did his wife feel any pangs of jealousy or distrust. It was simply an experiment on her part, and he used to chuckle immensely when he told me how perfectly it succeeded.

I shall now dismiss this subject, feeling that I have done my bare duty by my readers in thus glancing at, rather than fully describing, one of the most curious phases of my varied experiences, while I abstain from breaking my promise to my instructor. I dare say, if they are inclined to pursue the subject of black magic, they will find the means of gratifying their desire. There is, in fact, a secret society working at this very time in the great Metropolis, under the auspices of a man in a somewhat prominent public position. I am not an initiate; but there are a great many ladies in its ranks; and ladies, as we know, will talk. They profess to have devised adequate safeguards for the practice of black magic; but the little I know of this fraternity—against whom I have nothing to say—confirms the opinion drawn from my own slender experience, and leads me to quote, for the benefit of such as are inclined to go in for black magic, *Punch's* historic advice to young men about to marry: "*Don't.*"

I had the run of Mr. Hockley's library, and read voluminously; but it is rather of events than of reading I desire to speak at present.

It is interesting to learn how Mr. Hockley gained his first taste for and knowledge of occultism. He was, when quite a youth, assistant to Dendy, who is the "D——" alluded to in the following passage which forms the opening of Lord Lytton's "Zanoni":—

"It is possible that, among my readers, there may be a few not unacquainted with an old book-shop existing some years since in the neighbourhood of Covent Garden; I say a few, for certainly there was little enough to attract the many, in those precious volumes which the labour of a life had accumulated on the dusty shelves of my old friend D——. There were to be found no popular treatises, no entertaining romances, no histories, no travels, no 'Library for the People,' no 'Amusement for the Million.' But there, perhaps, throughout all Europe, the curious might discover the most notable collection, ever amassed by an enthusiast, of the works of Alchemist, Cabalist, and Astrologer. The owner had lavished a fortune in the purchase of unsaleable treasures."

My third Master was Samuel Carter Hall, who, with his gifted wife, so familiarly known as "Mrs. S. C. Hall," was residing in the parish where I was at that time taking clerical duty. Mr. Hall entered *con amore* on the task of converting the curate to those doctrines wherein himself and his wife were such ardent devotees.

The shape in which this Master put his teaching was quite different from that adopted by my other instructors. He had been, he said, reclaimed from utter unbelief to faith wholly and solely by the agency of this new revelation.

It was at Mr. Hall's house I met Daniel D. Home, who had indirectly been the means of my first inquiring into these matters; and at a very early period of my acquaintance with this remarkable personage I witnessed the phenomenon of "levitation."

We were sitting in the after-glow of a bright summer evening, the room being otherwise unlighted. Home had his back to the window, and I was sitting at the table exactly opposite to him. I could see him quite distinctly; and, after sundry other manifestations, I beheld him rise perpendicularly in the air. After he had risen some distance, and in evident unconsciousness that he had done so, he said, "I think I shall be levitated to-night." I told him he had already risen, and he again said, "No, but I think I shall." He then rose still higher until his feet were above the level of the table, when he turned gently over into a horizontal position and floated towards me with his toes steering straight for my nose. I asked him whether I should move, and he replied, "No; sit still. I shall clear you." He was then about eighteen inches above the table; and, as he passed me, he said, "Follow me and pass your hands above and below me." I assured him there was no necessity for this, as I had no suspicions; but he repeated, "Do as I tell you. I want you to be able to say you have done it." I followed him out into the darkness, and kept passing my hands above and below him, until he was floated right round the room, and then back, as buoyantly as a balloon, into his place again.

Now — as Robert Bell wrote — I do not

expect people of necessity to believe this. Possibly I was hypnotised, as might also have been my wife, our host and hostess, and the five or six other people present. Cranes and other cumbrous machinery I do not believe in. I think we should have seen them before or after the séance, and they would have looked altogether out of place in that elegantly furnished drawing-room.

If we were not hypnotised, that man was in space for several minutes, and I handled him while he was making the circuit of a fairly-sized room. There was nothing necessarily "spiritual" in the exhibition; but what had become of our good old gravitation and Sir Isaac Newton's apple?

This took place in semi-obscurity, true; but there was quite light enough to see all that was going on at the table, which was close to the window. Nor did the manifestations cease when the gas was lighted. Chairs came from one side of the room to the other; and there were no wires about, or we should have tumbled over them, for we moved about freely. Lady Dunsaney was one of those present; and her black lace shawl was violently pulled. Concluding that she was to take it off, she removed her brooch, when the shawl was whisked away and deposited in a heap on the table at which we had been sitting.

This had been almost my first experience of what are called physical manifestations. An accordion held in Home's hand was played upon, though we felt his other hand free; and many of us felt touches from unseen fingers on our faces. I remember thinking I should squirm horribly if this occurred to me; but I did not. I was quite ready to repeat the frequent request of the sitters—though not perhaps in quite the same words—"Do touch me again, dear spirits!" They were quite sure they were in contact with their departed friends. I was, I think, pretty well on towards the pneumatological explanation of the phenomena, but I was not quite prepared to identify the intelligences, or, at all events, to address them as "dears."

The use of that word "pneumatological" recalls to my mind the best treatise I have ever read on this branch of the subject. It was written by Professor De Morgan in the form of a preface to his wife's book "From Matter to Spirit," and I am not the least ashamed in company with such a man to confess that I was puzzled, and disposed to regard the "spiritual" theory as the easiest way out of the difficulty. The following is the passage that was recalled to my recollection by the use of the term in question :—

"I am perfectly convinced that I have both seen and heard, in a manner which should make unbelief impossible, things *called* spiritual which cannot be taken by a rational being to be capable of explanation by imposture, coincidence, or mistake. So far I feel the ground firm under me.

But when it comes to what is the cause of these phenomena, I find I cannot adopt any explanation which has yet been suggested. If I were bound to choose among things which I can conceive, I should say that there is some sort of action of some combination of will, intellect, and physical power, which is not that of any of the human beings present. But thinking it very likely that the universe may contain a few agencies—say half a million—about which no man knows anything, I cannot but suspect that a small proportion of these agencies—say five thousand—may be severally competent to the production of all the phenomena, or may be quite up to the task among them. The physical explanations which I have seen are easy, but miserably insufficient; the spiritual hypothesis is sufficient, but ponderously difficult."

The forty-five pages which Professor De Morgan prefixed to his wife's book make up, to my thinking, the very best treatise ever put forth on this singularly vexed question; and I have often suggested to my transcendental friends the advisability of getting permission to print them as a pamphlet. But no; the Professor is not "grim" enough. Moreover, he looks at both sides—an unpardonable sin in the estimation of those who can, or will, only see one side.

On his last page but one, after a brief narrative of the "staggerers" which have come under his notice, Professor De Morgan thus concludes, in terms so jocular as to ensure his being put out of court by the grim people:—

"The things which I have narrated were the beginning of a long series of experiences; many as remarkable as what I have given; many of a minor character, separately worth little, but of a character not sustentive of the gravity and dignity of the spiritual world. The celebrated apparition of Giles Scroggins is a serious personage compared to some which have fallen in my way, and a logical one too. If these things be spirits, they show that pretenders, coxcombs, and liars are to be found on the other side of the grave as well as on this; and what for no? as Meg Dodds said."

These were the three Masters, then, under whose guidance I gained my earliest acquaintance with the wider range of occult studies. They were men of widely different types; and two out of the three, one would have been slow to credit with any disposition towards transcendentalism. They have long since passed away, and I can speak of them without reserve. Benjamin Coleman was decidedly of the aggressive order. Frederick Hockley was the quiet, patient student. Samuel Carter Hall, the typical transcendentalist, with his Irish impulsiveness and his boundless capacity of belief, rather overacted his part, and was only prevented from degenerating into still further eccentricities by the influence of his gifted wife, who, although as devout a believer as himself, knew better than he did how to temper her zeal with discretion.

Of Daniel Home, to whom I was introduced by the Halls, I can only write as I found him. I have since had a large experience with professional mediums, and he is one of the few about whom I can say with confidence that I never had the shadow of a doubt. Professional, in the technical sense of the term, he was not; for I believe he never took money for his mediumistic gifts. Of course it will be urged that he gained notoriety, even if he did not pocket current coin of the realm. The case of Lyon v. Home will be quoted, which turned upon a silly old woman giving him a large fortune and then taking it back again. With this I have nothing to do. I only speak of his good faith so far as I could test it under circumstances where he came in contact with myself. I cannot too often repeat that this is merely a collection of personal reminiscences. Looking back over all that lapse of years, I feel that, even in my early discipleship, I kept my eyes and ears well open, and neither the one nor the other ever caused me to have the slightest suspicion of Daniel Home. My suspicions of others might have been groundless. I am speaking only of those whose performances appeared to violate the known laws of nature, not those whose gifts, like those of Emma Hardinge, amounted only to an exaltation of natural faculties.

My range soon widened. I found new Masters with fresh ministers; but those I have named were the three who met me at the vestibule of the temple, and passed me on to the interior for more formal initiation.

CHAPTER VI

OCCULTISM IN ITS HOMELY ASPECTS

> " I doubt it would not render angels blest
>   To be concerned in all our mean affairs ;
> Nor would the souls of men find peace and rest
>   In being over-conversant with theirs.
>
> So pressing the concerns of daily life,
>   So hardly taxed our energies to gain
> The bread which perishes, that studies rife
>   With spirit-rapture would engender pain,
>
> And half unfit us for our earthly sphere ;
>   And therefore angel visits rarely break
> On human vision ; rarely spirits cheer
>   The lonely walks that sad survivors take."
>   —J. C. EARLE
>   (*The Spiritual Body*).

ONE of the most striking volumes of sermons I ever read had for its title "Christianity in its Homely Aspects." The discourses were designed to bring their subject down from the transcendental heights of theology to the level of daily experience, and so to prevent it being, as it too often is, "from man's life a thing apart." It was under this aspect that the new revelation—if such it should prove to be—so strongly arrested my attention. What if it should prove to be the missing link in the golden chain, and destined to make Christianity, as the Article of the Church quaintly expresses it, "understanded of the people"?

By this I did *not* mean to degrade the office of the intelligences down to the low level contemplated in such books as "Spirit-workers in the Home Circle," where the supposed spirits lighted the kitchen fire, and did the domestic work generally, in a way not quite so satisfactory as a general servant. But if the theory so far enunciated should prove to be sound, every home might have its "circle;" and that, according to the Rev. H. R. Haweis, means its own "church." He sets aside the ordinary etymology of the word "church," which, he assures us, is not derived from the Greek word signifying "the Lord's house," but simply from the common

Latin noun "circus" meaning "circle." If it be true that the third letter of the alphabet was sounded hard by the Romans, one only has to remove the Latin termination and there is the word "kirk" ready made. Was the circle in the large upper room where the apparitions of the Risen Christ occurred, being revived in our midst?

The first of these "homely aspects" to which I shall draw attention had a sort of ecclesiastical tinge about it. I used to preach occasionally at the Church of All Saints, Notting Hill, and my occult proclivities must have begun to be talked about; for one Sunday evening the verger who waited upon me in the vestry told me that his brother, a carpenter in an adjacent street, in conjunction with certain other "rude mechanicals," rented a loft over a stable near the Latimer Road Station on the Metropolitan Railway, where they held frequent séances, and would be very glad to see me if I cared to be present.

I took an early opportunity of going to the place indicated, and was greatly impressed by what I saw. These good people were thoroughly in earnest. There was a large gathering of working-men, their wives and daughters—some of the latter quite young girls; and they always opened their proceedings with prayer, singing frequent hymns during the sitting. The manifestations were exceedingly strong, not to say violent, but never offensive in any way. The fluency with which some of the girls poured forth extempore prayers, and these simple working-men delivered addresses, formed quite a new phase of the subject for me; I frequently attended these meetings, and took with me others who were interested in the religious aspect of occultism.

I also paid a visit to a Mrs. Olive who lived in a little back street at Islington, and whom I had heard highly spoken of as a trance-medium. This form of manifestation was then comparatively new to me; though I cannot say I was at first greatly attracted to it. Of course, the orations at Beethoven Rooms were supposed to be of this character; but even such a copious power of extemporaneous oratory was not altogether abnormal, though exceedingly curious, and occasionally past all explanation, except that of thought-reading, when the speakers dealt with matters of fact entirely beyond their own knowledge. A case of this kind occurred immediately when I visited Mrs. Olive.

She passed at once into a trance, and addressed me in words belonging to a personality other than her own. She had been with me all that afternoon, she said—for the personality was still feminine—and she was so sorry for that poor drowned man.

"What drowned man?" I asked, for I was not conscious of having kept company with a corpse.

"Yes, you have," she replied. "You have got his book in your pocket now."

Then I understood. I had recently met a

person closely related to Shelley's companion when he was drowned, and I had been reading the account of the catastrophe in a narrative prefixed to Shelley's works. I had the book in my pocket, and that was the drowned man to whom this medium's *locum tenens* referred.

Mrs. Olive is, I believe, still acting as a medium; but she lost her first husband, married again, and is now Madame Greck.

An incident of a similar character occurred with the American medium, Fletcher. I met him at a house in Kensington, and he said that a spirit of one who had been a clergyman was anxious to communicate with me. Of course, I asked who it was; and he said he could see the name written down, but did not like to read it, because it must be wrong.

I told him to go on, and he read—

"C. A. N.—Oh, no!" he exclaimed, "it is nonsense.—O. N.," he proceeded, eventually giving the whole name as "Canon Kingsley."

The first place, however, where I heard the

"spirit-voice" proper was at the Marshalls', in Bristol Gardens, Maida Hill. For some time this family, consisting of mother, son, and the latter's wife, had a monopoly of what the elder lady termed "sperrits." They were very "homely" people indeed; the mother and daughter-in-law being mediums, and the male Marshall playing the fiddle, while a large round table danced. On my first visit I went alone, paid my fee, and sat at the table, asking questions when it came to my turn. I am sure nobody present knew me; but the names of my father and the little boy I had lost were correctly given, as also the cemetery where the latter was buried. I asked for some message from my father which should serve to identify him to me, and the following oracular sentence was spelt out—

"Do not hide your light under a bushel."

I cannot say that this paternal injunction carried conviction with it; but it forms a good specimen of the sort of twaddle one has to put up with in the intervals of intelligent replies, which are frequently few and far between.

On the occasion of my second visit, I played a little trick. I sent my wife on before with a barrister friend, and afterwards came in alone, taking my place at the table and treating the wife of my bosom and her escort as perfect strangers. My wife asked the communicating intelligence to spell out her name, and it tried to do so, but bungled.

After the light séance, we went into a back room and sat in the dark for the voices.

They came at once. "John King," supposed to have been a bold buccaneer during his earthly and maritime life, spoke in stentorian tones, and the first remark he made to me, after addressing me by name, was—

"What did you play us that trick for? Why didn't you say she was your wife?"

My wife had, of course, preserved her incognito up to this point.

Then came a whispered voice supposed to

belong to "Katie King," which by-and-by addressed my wife in a confidential way, begging her not to trouble herself about my acquaintance with "those people."

"What people?" my wife naturally asked, for she was thinking of none at the time.

The whispered voice named them. They were a family with whom I had recently become acquainted, and whom my wife did not think very eligible, but had never mentioned the matter to me or any one. The whispered voice, however, had the name pat, and added—

"You need not trouble yourself about it; the acquaintance will be a short one." And, as a fact, this proved to be the case.

There was nothing very edifying in the discourse of John King; and it required a strong effort to dissociate the voice from possible connection with the male performer in the trio. One sceptical sitter even deposed to smelling a savour of onions when the whispered voice came very close. The darkness was, of course, unsatisfactory. It was as likely to suggest suspicion as to encourage fraud. The scientist has no right to complain of this possibly necessary condition until he can conduct his spectrum analysis in full light.

On a third occasion I went to the Marshalls', accompanied by a Catholic priest. I had been telling him my experiences; and he, of course, held that they were diabolical.

"I could stop them at once," he said, "if I carried some holy water with me and silently pronounced the words of exorcism."

I begged him to come and try; and after some persuasion he consented to do so. He would not sit at the table, but on a sofa at some distance; and it was arranged that when matters were in full swing he should give me a private sign that he was exorcising and holy-watering.

I asked only one question, and that was that the name of a person about whom I was thinking should be spelt out for me. This was done—three names belonging to an exceedingly clever poetess recently dead. She was by no means a "spiritual" person, and her letters were always particularly smart and incisive. I said—

"To prove that it is really you yourself communicating, give me a characteristic message such as you used to write."

The message that came was, "I am saved, and will now save others."

This, again, was scarcely conclusive as a criterion; and, soon after, my ecclesiastical friend gave me the sign that he was operating.

Bearing in mind what my Master had told me about the superfluous character of the adjuncts in spells—among which I was disrespectful enough to include the holy water and the form of exorcism—I determined to exercise my will that the manifestations should go on. But it was no use. They stopped dead; and after a while Mrs. Marshall, senior, was fain to remark—

"'The sperrits is gone. I heard their feet a-patterin' away jest now."

As a matter of fact, they had gone, though we did not hear the pattering footfalls. No more communications were received that evening, and the priest was jubilant.

In consequence of the reputation I had gained for dealing with mesmerism in particular, and occult matters in general, I frequently received visits from strangers who wished to consult me on the subject. A lady called and said her daughter had been playing at the game of "willing," and had failed to do what she was "willed" by one of her companions. She had successfully resisted the inclination, and had ever since been in a nervous condition, which had now extended over several weeks. She felt that this companion's influence was still on the recalcitrant young damsel, and would be greatly obliged if I would lay my hands on the young lady's head and remove that influence. I told her that young ladies' heads were very delicate things to deal with, and that I must decline to operate. Indeed, so far as my experience went, the only person who could remove the influence would be the one who had imposed it, and I therefore referred her back to the young companion whose behest had been disobeyed.

I had indeed often seen this exemplified in my own patient. She would make up her mind to rebel, and resist an inclination which she felt was due to my suggestion; but she invariably had to "cave in." Life became a burden until she had done what she was told, or until I had released her from her promise.

Another visitor of the same kind was a French gentleman, master in a large suburban school, who had recently enjoyed what might be described as "A Week with a Ghost." He had lost a favourite child, a little girl, and went with his wife to a photographer's to arrange for the enlargement of his daughter's carte-de-visite portrait. The assistant was a young lady who afterwards became a famous medium; and as she was even then beginning to develop her faculty, she told the grief-stricken parents that she could put them into communication with their lost darling. She did so there and then; and when they went back to their shadowed home, they renewed the intercourse through the medium of the table. Little loving messages came, and they felt that the child was really with them again. The father was evidently a powerful physical medium; and for a week that table walked their quarters like a thing of life—if one may so paraphrase a familiar line. Then, all at once, it occurred to the father that he might be deceived. He was a devout Catholic, and believed in the potency of exorcism as firmly as my friend the priest. He pronounced the name of the Trinity and adjured the intelligence—

"Are you the spirit of our daughter?"

The table was lifted beneath their hands, and came down with one decisive thump.

"No!"

"Who are you?" Again with the same adjuration.

"Le Diable!"

Here all communications were at once discontinued. The gentleman had put his experiences into writing, and wished me to look over the MS. before publication. I did so, and the pamphlet is even still well known in the bibliography of this particular form of occultism.

I often met with this inquirer afterwards; for he could not resist the temptation to communicate even with the undesirable personage who constantly asserted his presence. My acquaintance with this French gentleman extended over some years, and I shall have occasion again to mention him in connection with my own excursion into the realms of *diablerie*. Towards the end of his life, however, he discontinued all such forbidden pursuits, and died at last in the odour of sanctity.

The name of this gentleman would be at once recognised if I dared give it. I only suppress it in consideration for his survivors.

It may seem perhaps almost a misnomer to call my next incident by the name of a "homely" aspect, since in this case our visitants found their warmest welcome at an inn. Mrs. Berry had taken that highly respectable caravanserai the Hyde Park Hotel, opposite the Marble Arch; and being an ardent devotee of the New Faith herself, gave sittings once a week, to which I was invited, and which I regularly attended. No one can accuse me of Laodiceanism or lukewarmness at this period, since I had been sitting for nearly a year of Wednesdays for several hours in blank darkness with very slender results indeed, insomuch that I am astonished at my own patience, for I am sure I could not do it now. True, the séance was followed by a *recherché* little supper, at which we met nice people and ate nice things—the choicest the hotel could produce. We used to sit at separate round tables; and the jovial hostess was a little disappointed if some of these did not gyrate during supper, which they generally did. We had several mediums on most occasions. Perhaps we had too many, and one influence counteracted the other. The results were certainly incommensurate with the time devoted. Amongst others, I remember an old man named Cogman, who used to go off into a trance and talk gibberish, as we unlearned ones used to think—much as the unbelieving Jews did on the day of Pentecost. One night, however, Mr. Alfred Russel Wallace, author of "The Malay Archipelago" and "Travels on the Amazon," was present. He assured me that it was no gibberish, but a regular language. He bade me note the recurrence of certain sounds, and said he knew it was the language of some part of Polynesia, though he failed to "fix" it exactly. Of course, I could not contradict him. Mr. Wallace is also the author of one of the best books on this form of occultism; it is entitled "The Scientific Aspect of the Supernatural," and his name, of course, carries weight with it, seeing that he divides with Darwin the honour of having formulated the doctrine of Evolution. Seeing that the occultists had at this time Mr. Wallace and Professor Crookes on their side, the materialists could not boast of monopolising the big men.

I began, I confess, to get a little tired of these Hyde Park Hotel gatherings, despite the *recherché* character of the suppers. I was lolling back in my chair one night—in blank darkness, remember—and feeling that time was being wasted. I kept my hands on the table, however, and suddenly a very small soft hand was laid on mine. It felt like the hand of a big child or a small girl; I recollect thinking it was like what my boy Charlie's— an imp of twelve—would be, only it was soft and felt clean, which Charlie's at that period seldom was. I was determined not to be fooled, so I said nothing, but cast about me as to who was sitting near. My neighbours on either side were Mrs. Marshall the younger and Mr. Cogman, neither of them having very small hands; in fact, nobody in the room had. Still I held my peace, and only whispered, "May I turn my hand over?" Three gentle taps from those velvet-like fingers formed the response. I turned my hand over, and the little hand was laid confidingly in mine. When I attempted to close my hand it appeared to melt away. After a time I said, still beneath my breath, "Can you take off my ring?" Again came three raps on my hand. I wear my ring, a large intaglio, on the fourth finger of the right hand, and it fits very tightly, so that it is difficult to get off. I felt the tiny nails working down under that refractory ring; but eventually the task was accomplished.

When I got home, I asked my wife to write automatically in reply to my question.

Without telling her what had occurred, I asked who was present. Our dead child's name was given, and he said that he could now communicate himself, adding—

"I always go with you to séances."

"But, Johnny," I rejoined, "that was not you to-night?"

"No," he replied; "it was Charlie's turn."

"Charlie's turn!" we said; "what *do* you mean?"

The last word was rewritten almost petulantly, with a very much emphasised dot in the proper place. "Charlie's *twin*."

Charlie, be it remarked, was one of twins, his twin-brother being still-born; and it had occurred to me that the hand was about the size of Charlie's.

But how came it that both the writer and myself misread the word? That seems to do away completely with the idea of unconscious cerebration. The same number of strokes serves for either word; it is the dot that makes the difference. But surely if we had expected the word "twin," we should have written it plainly, or, at all events, have read it correctly when written.

It is little isolated incidents like this which serve to correct our crude theories, suggesting that we have not got quite to the bottom of the Modern Mystery yet.

My final incident under this heading again takes me to what had been a large hotel in the western suburbs, but which had been "converted" (like myself), and was now my school. It was a great big rambling place, and on several occasions we had heard uncanny noises during the small hours, though we were generally too busy or too tired to take much notice of them. I had often prowled about the staircases at night, on the look-out, not for spirits, but for mischievous boarders who, I fancied, were skylarking. The noise seemed always in front of me; I never could overtake it. At last I got tired of acting Demetrius and Lysander to a possible Puck, so I let the wanderers wander at their own sweet will.

More than once, too, the children, when they were small and slept in the juniors' dormitory next to our bedroom, came scared to our bedside in the middle of the night. They were unable or unwilling to say what they had seen or heard; but they were terribly frightened at something. Then, again, different generations of servants, who could not by any possibility have communicated with each other, would come with a story of a tall lady in a rustling black silk dress who roamed the topmost corridor, on to which their bedrooms opened. By-and-by some of the neighbours began to ask whether it was possible I did not know the place was "troubled" when I took it. Old inhabitants could remember when it was familiarly called "The Haunted House."

In course of time we left it, not on account of the "troublings," which would have rather enhanced its value to us in our then state of mind. The last van-load of furniture had gone, when a maid-servant who had been upstairs packing her boxes came to me, her face green with terror, and told me she had seen a tall lady dressed in black, and was sure it was a ghost.

"Very likely it is," I replied; "and the poor ghost wants to say something to us before we go."

Not for a hundred pounds would that terrified domestic go upstairs again, she said. She would rather leave all her things behind, &c. How she managed eventually to get her effects off I do not know; but I resolved I would interview that ghost if possible.

I had recently met Kate Fox, the heroine of the "Rochester Knockings," in America, and she had promised to give me a sitting. She was then married to Mr. Jencken, a barrister. So off I went and arranged a séance for that evening. I got a table and some chairs carried back, for we were only moving into the next street, and then invited six or seven people to join us, of course without telling Mrs. Jencken or any of them what had taken place. Fortunately among my sitters I had invited another "seeing medium" as a sort of understudy, since I knew my American friend was a little erratic in her movements. She never turned up; but the understudy fortunately proved equal to the occasion. This was a Mrs. Wiseman, who lived in a square close by.

When we had sat a short time in the moonlight and heard all sorts of mysterious bangings of doors, &c., in the empty house, Mrs. Wiseman started, and whispered to me, "Do you see?"

I saw nothing, and told her so, asking what *she* saw.

"A tall girl—very tall—dressed in black. She walks round the circle repeatedly, and every time she comes to you she stops, as though she wanted to speak to you."

Unfortunately neither my wife nor any writing medium was present, and we could not get either raps or tilts; so that when we broke up, nobody, with the single exception of Mrs. Wiseman, had seen anything at all.

At Mrs. Wiseman's house, however, was a lady who wrote automatically, and we requested her to tell us who our mysterious visitor was, and what she wanted to say to me. Her name, we were told, was Helen Klein. She had been staying in that hotel, and was murdered by a man, whose name I have forgotten. She was to have been married to him, and was still so amiably disposed that she wished him to have a small sum of money which was in her possession when she died. I was to be the means of getting the money for him.

I did not feel at all inclined to undertake the task, and went home without probing deeply into the matter.

But my curiosity was roused. When I got home I asked my wife to write and tell me whether the details were correctly given.

Not quite, I was informed. The girl's name was "Ada Klein," not "Helen Klein"

—no name, be it remarked, having been mentioned by me, or any particulars given. She wished the man, whose name was repeated, to have the money, and begged that I would get it for her. She named the church in the churchyard of which she was buried, and said I should find her name on the register of burials there, giving the date. The church, however, was one at which I frequently officiated, and I had no excuse for asking to see the registers, whilst I was unwilling to give the real reason. I asked how it was the matter was not made public, and the reply given was that her death was attributed to a fit. Inquests, I was told, in reply to a further question, were not so regularly held then as now.

It was a lame and impotent conclusion, requiring verification only to make a good blood-curdling ghost story. The curious element was the two automatic writers giving the names and event without any information from me or communication with each other.

If I may venture to forecast the future, in spite of the wholesome maxim not to prophesy unless you know, it seems to me that it is under this homely aspect the special form of occultism with which I have been dealing is likely to remain after the subsidence of what I have called the wave of supernaturalism. Unfortunately for themselves, but perhaps fortunately for the community, few of the public mediums who have made a profession of occultism have escaped detection in certain malpractices. Society has itself to thank for being duped. People pay exorbitant fees to mediums for the sake of showing off a nine days' wonder to their friends, and are disappointed if they do not get results. Now, the medium cannot command results, and he knows it, so he comes prepared for emergencies. Where a man is in an independent position, as D. D. Home was, and especially when he knows his sitters will not be staggered by absence of phenomenal results, there is no temptation, and a man would not run the chances of detection unless absolutely driven to it. I have sat a whole evening with Home when Professor Crookes used a craftily devised apparatus for measuring the amount of force brought to bear by the unseen power, and not a manifestation of any kind occurred. On another occasion results followed at once. When we take young people from humble positions, and tempt them by payment of a guinea or two guineas an evening to exhibit the powers they occasionally possess, we tempt them to eke out their powers with fraud. I have over and over again seen instances of this. People who undoubtedly possessed occult power palpably played tricks. They could not afford to fail. At one of the Hyde Park Hotel gatherings, where, as I said, the hostess felt aggrieved if a table or two did not pirouette at supper, I saw one of them commence a hornpipe, and from the position in which I was sitting I could see the occupant, an undoubted medium, doing the whole business with her foot. I did not denounce her as a fraud; but I leapt up suddenly, and with unaccustomed politeness handed her a plate of something. I looked at her foot and then at her face, in a way that plainly conveyed to her, "If you don't stop, I'll tell." Down went the foot, the pirouetting suddenly ceased, and was not renewed that evening.

One of the best séances I remember was held at my own house without a professional medium. The sitters were myself, my wife, a delicate girl engaged to one of my family, and her mother. This girl had laughed at me because I set aside a room in my house for hocus-pocus; but she had been convinced, and then brought her mother, who had been also inclined to jeer. The father, who had been dead some years, was a medical man in large practice at the West End; and, though not an habitual church-goer, was accustomed, as I only learned after his death, to attend the services at which I preached as Sunday evening lecturer. I did not know him even by sight; but, after his death, analyses of my sermons were found in his commonplace book. Possibly this did not say much for the worthy doctor's discrimination, but so it was. He purported to communicate with us, and named his daughter, Constance, as a medium. When his widow attended under the circumstances I have mentioned, he made a communication to her which was quite unintelligible to all of us, but served to convince her that it could come from no one but her departed husband. At this séance we had the bright points of brilliant light, like that of magnesium, floating about in the darkness. I confess I had always had my suspicions of these lights, which, of course, could be easily produced by a trickster; but there were no conjurers here, even if there had been any possible motive for trickery. A large column of misty light as tall as a man, too, appeared quite distinctly, though the windows were closely covered with American cloth tacked tightly down.

My brother—not the one who acted showman in Paris, but a fairly 'cute, hard-headed lawyer—died whilst I was in the thick of my investigations. He had always denounced occultism, saying he had too much to believe already without adding that. He died of a disease which left him in full possession of his faculties to the very last. When he felt himself dying, he begged I might be telegraphed for; but his request was not granted until it was too late. Then he said to my other brother—the showman—who was alone with him: "Tell him," naming me, "when he comes, that I wanted to shake him by the hand and to tell him that *it is all true*. They are telling me to say this. They seem to be writing it on blocks as it were, and I read it off." Then he would speak of ordinary matters, and by-and-by exclaim, "Now they are going to talk again." By the time I reached his bedside he had lost consciousness; in fact, he was to all intents and purposes dead.

One confirmation gained thus in a quarter where suspicion is impossible is worth any number paid for at so much an hour.

Let me be just, however. Perhaps the very strongest testimony I ever had as to the reality of the phenomena was given by Rita, a professional medium in a séance held at Captain James's. The slate-writing mania, as it was termed, was then in full swing. I bought a new folding-slate, put the orthodox crumb of slate-pencil inside, gummed paper over the edges, tied it up with string and put sealing-wax over the knots. In the evening I produced the slate. Rita simply held one corner of it, and I gripped the other three-quarters firmly. The slate never left my possession for the fraction of a second; but we heard the bit of pencil working inside, and when we cut the fastenings we found written inside, "God bless you all!"

No more. The intelligence was epigrammatic as Tiny Tim himself; but would not have been more convincing if it had transcribed the whole of the 119th Psalm.

"There, Mr. Maskelyne," I once said to that excellent conjurer; "you could not produce writing under those conditions. I know how you do your slate-writing, because Dr. Sexton 'exposed' your legerdemain. But you could not do it so, could you?"

"Not supposing you have stated the conditions correctly," he said; meaning, of course, to imply that I had *not*—that I had been fooled in some way or other. But I repeat, unless I was a good way into the hypnotic borderland, I never let go of that slate, and the rest who were present saw me holding on like grim death. Yet there was the writing "plain for all folk to see."

It was a homely aspect enough, but a very staggering one, and I can see only one explanation of it. The others—including the Egyptian Hall process, which is enormously clever—fail to cover the facts.

CHAPTER VII

MRS. GRUNDY'S ANATHEMA

"Be quiet woolye? Always ding, dinging Dame Grundy into my ears. 'What will Mrs. Grundy say? What will Mrs. Grundy think?' Casn't thee be quiet, let her alone, and behave thyself pratty? ... I do verily think when thee goest to t'other world, the vurst question thee't ax will be, if Mrs. Grundy's there. Zoa be quiet, and behave pratty, doo'e. ... Dom Mrs. Grundy!" —*Speed the Plough.*

UP to a certain point I had quite omitted to put the question suggested by the satirist: "But what is your opinion, Mrs. Grundy?"

I own it had never occurred to me that occultism, as I had known or practised it, could possibly be *per se* wrong. It might be wise or unwise to trouble one's self about it, judicious or injudicious to acknowledge one's self a possible convert—I had been warned betimes as to the unwisdom; but I could not, and, I am afraid I must put it in the present tense by adding, I cannot see, that it is any violation of good morals to "go in" for white magic. Black magic is quite a different matter; and I hold no brief for that.

Other people, however, thought differently. I found I was beginning to be regarded as a "dangerous" man. You have to be a parson, or in a parsonic set, to know exactly what that means.

A nice old motherly incumbent of a West End church met the holder of an adjoining benefice, on whose list of preachers my name appeared; and pointing to it solemnly with his inevitable umbrella, he asked, "Why have you got *him?*" "Why should I not?" asked the other, who was rather an advanced man— a *fin de siècle* doctor of divinity; and then the maternal one said with added solemnity, "He is a *dangerous* man."

Possibly this refutation brought about my somewhat abrupt removal from the parish church where I had officiated for several years, though I do not know that this was the case; and I only moved to a daughter church in the same parish, the incumbent of which latter was a thorough believer in occultism; but he was wise in his generation, and veiled his belief *à la Nicodemus*.

Probably the reason why the motherly party hoisted the danger signal was not merely the fact that I openly acknowledged my occult studies, but the additional one that the Dialectical Society had appointed a committee to investigate the Modern Mystery, and I had on that account frequently attended meetings of the society while Mr. Bradlaugh sat on the committee in question. I know for a fact that this was the stumbling-block; for one day my new incumbent, to whose Sunday evening lectureship I had been recently appointed, told me, with a merry twinkle of the eye, that he had met one of the usual congregation steering away from church, and on being asked why he did so, replied that the new evening lecturer attended meetings of a society which numbered Mr. Bradlaugh amongst its members.

"You can do without him," said the incumbent. "There is a remarkably good congregation."

I doubt whether the orthodoxy of each member in the Psychical Research Society at the present day would bear too severe a test; but I think a harmless parson might belong to it without being therefore labelled "Dangerous," except by the very straitest of Mrs. Grundy's adherents.

On the committee of the Dialectical Society itself, in close alphabetical proximity to Mr. Bradlaugh, was the name of a doctor of divinity, though I grant that he had closely identified himself with the study of unorthodoxy in general; and perhaps his ægis would scarcely suffice to ward off the darts of Dame Grundy. The society took the very broadest basis; but its examination into the pros and cons of the Modern Mystery was searching and satisfactory, and the report it formulated has now attained the dignity of an historical document.

This document was as long-winded as though it had itself come straight from the spheres. It was highly favourable, so far as the genuineness of the manifestations was concerned ; and the gist of the whole matter was summed up in the concluding paragraph :

"In presenting their report, your committee, taking into consideration the high character and great intelligence of many of the witnesses to the more extraordinary facts, the extent to which their testimony is supported by the reports of the sub-committees, and the absence of any proof of imposture or delusion as regards a large portion of the phenomena ; and, further, having regard to the exceptional character of the phenomena, the large number of persons in every grade of society and over the whole civilised world who are more or less influenced by a belief in their supernatural origin, and to the fact that no philosophical explanation of them has yet been arrived at—deem it incumbent upon them to state their conviction that the subject is worthy of more serious attention and careful investigation than it has hitherto received."

It was the old story of Balaam over again. The Dialectical Society were called in to curse the occultists, and, lo! they had blessed them altogether. A very large number of the Dialecticians were converted in the process of examining evidence, and some of them turned out strong mediums.

The sub-committees sat in circle at the residences of the different members, inviting others who belonged to the society, or had attended its meetings, to join them. In most cases the gatherings were quiet enough; but I was present at the sitting of a sub-committee at the house of the only clerical member of the committee, which nearly ended in a shindy. The medium in this case was a relative of the host, and one of the members, a rather noisy vestry-meeting kind of orator, wished to impose some very rigorous tests upon the lady. The ecclesiastic in question chose to regard this as a reflection on his relative's veracity, and the way in which he drove that demagogic gentleman out of his house reminded one of the row upon the Stanislaus as related by Truthful James, who thus moralises:—

> "Now I hold it is not decent for a scientific gent
> To say another is an ass—at least, to all intent;
> Nor should the individual who happens to be meant
> Reply by heaving rocks at him to any great extent."

But Mrs. Grundy was not happy. The constitution of the Dialectical Society was based on the principle that nothing should be accepted save as the conclusion of a logical argument; and Mrs. G. hastened to anathematise the whole affair — both the heterodox society and the heresy—as she deemed it—which they thus patted on the back.

The leading scientific men of the day were invited to the meetings of the Dialectical

Society's Committee; and the replies they sent were very characteristic. I am not quite sure whether these representative scientists were more angry with the hanky-panky people, or with the Socratic Society which assumed to act umpire. They certainly were angry with somebody.

It is, I am afraid, an index of an ill-regulated condition of mind on my part; but when I find people getting angry and riding the high horse in this way, I am sure to be reminded irresistibly of some mock-heroic Hudibrastic kind of utterance or other; and in face of these stilted refusals from the leaders in science, there flashed on my memory some replies from certain poets quoted by Mr. W. S. Gilbert in his poem called "Ferdinando and Elvira," which forms one of the well-known "Bab Ballads." The heroine, Elvira, is seized with a burning desire to know who it is that writes those lovely mottoes inside the Christmas crackers; and her Ferdinando, by way of unearthing the bard, puts the demand boldly to those "leading poets" Mr. Close and Mr. Martin Tupper, with the following result:—

"Mister Close expressed a wish that he could only get anigh to me.
And Mister Martin Tupper sent the following reply to me:—
'A fool is bent upon a twig, but wise men dread a bandit.'
Which, of course, was very clever; but I didn't understand it."

Really the following replies from the "leading scientists" were much of the same order. Especially of the latter was it true that, though of course it must be very clever, nobody could understand it.

I.

"SIR,—I regret that I am unable to accept the invitation of the Council of the Dialectical Society to co-operate with a committee for the investigation of 'spiritualism;' and for two reasons. In the first place, I have no time for such an inquiry, which would involve much trouble and (unless it were unlike all inquiries of that kind I have known) much annoyance. In the second place, I take no interest in the subject. The only case of 'spiritualism' I have had the opportunity of examining into for myself was as gross an imposture as ever came under my notice. But supposing the phenomena to be genuine—they do not interest me. If anybody would endow me with the faculty of listening to the chatter of old women and curates in the nearest cathedral town, I should decline the privilege, having better things to do.

"And if the folk in the spiritual world do not talk more wisely and sensibly than their friends report them to do, I put them in the same category.

"The only good that I can see in a demonstration of the truth of 'spiritualism' is to furnish an additional argument against suicide. Better live a crossing-sweeper than die to be made to talk twaddle by a 'medium' hired at a guinea a séance.—I am, Sir, &c.,   T. H. HUXLEY.

"*29th January* 1869."

II.

"DEAR SIR,—I shall not be able to attend the investigation of 'spiritualism;' and in reference to your question about suggestions, would only say that the one hint needful is that all present should distinguish between facts and inferences from facts. When any man says that phenomena are produced by *no* known physical laws, he declares that he knows the laws by which they are produced. —Yours, &c.,   G. H. LEWES.

"*Tuesday, 2nd February* 1869."

But I must leave the Dialectical Society, adding only the remark that their report is well worth studying in full, and formed quite an epoch in the history of the movement, giving it for the moment a quasi-respectable character outside the charmed circle of Mrs. Grundy and the scientists— for the Pharisees and Herodians are always ready to join hands, and even include a sympathetic Sadducee or two when there is anything unpalatable they want to stamp out. The Psychical Research Society scarcely occupies the same position; but it will be time enough to show the points of difference when I speak of the latter body in due sequence. I come back now to my own purely personal experiences; though, after all, I shared to some extent in the proceedings of the society, as Mrs. Grundy found out.

The following incident, I think, brought the matter home as closely as anything to my own consciousness, excepting, of course, the loss of my own child.

A young lady in my congregation was seized with consumption, and her case promised to be a very rapid one. Member after member of her family had been swept off by the same disease; but, as is so often the case, this girl, whom it will be sufficient for me to name "Minnie," had not the slightest idea that she was suffering from anything but a severe cold. We could see her fading daily away, while the doctor, having pronounced the case hopeless and the end in all probability close at hand, felt she ought to be told. Her parents shrank from the task, and did not like to let it come as it were professionally from the medical man; so I was deputed to make the terrible announcement. We had often talked of these matters, and now I was to bring my theories to their most practical test. Walking in the garden amid the sunshine of a late autumn morning, I had to check some plans for the future by telling this young creature, for whom life seemed opening so pleasantly, that she must die—die *very soon!* She bore the tidings with perfect complacency, however; and we at once began to talk about the bearings of this new revelation on the Great Secret she was going to solve.

Minnie soon took to her bed, and I visited her daily. She liked nothing better than for me to bring one of my own children with me. The "reigning favourite" was then a tiny girl, who would sit on the bed while Minnie and I talked. She lasted somewhat longer than we expected, for I recollect the ringers were practising their Christmas peal at the parish church hard by, and suddenly Minnie made my little one start up from her picture-book and open her great brown eyes, by exclaiming—

"Oh, how glorious to think that I shall be in Heaven on Christmas Day!"

By-and-by she grew so weak that she could not raise herself in bed, but had to wait until I came to lift her. Then she liked to rest her head for a while on my shoulder. I had a notion that she got some of my superfluous vitality in that way; but she soon grew weary, and I had to lay her down again.

Then came the end. We saw it was very near; and it was arranged that I should administer the last Communion on Monday morning. On Sunday night, however, she felt she was dying, and begged I might be sent for. This was not the first time she had alarmed them thus; and as her parents thought I should be tired after my Sunday work, and knew I was coming early the next morning, they did not send. She lay moaning, "Do send for him. I want him to lift me;" and she died during that night. When I came in the morning I found her gone into closer "communion" than any she could have secured here.

On the Wednesday evening I went to my usual séance, and once or twice I could have declared I heard Minnie's whispered voice in the darkness. But I was still so much on my guard against the tricks of a "strong imagination" that I said nothing, though the hissing sound of that whispered voice came over and over again, and Minnie's speech had been almost inarticulate during the last few days before she passed away.

Minnie was to be buried on the Saturday; and on Friday evening I went to a séance in Bloomsbury with a lady who wanted me to test a young female medium just arrived from America.

After a good deal of talk between other members of the circle and those who claimed to be departed friends, there came the whispered voice again, and all heard it now. It was announced that the communication was for me, and that it came from "Minnie."

"What do you want to say?" I asked.

Then followed a whispered message which I could not hear. It was repeated, but was still inaudible to me. A stranger, however, who was closer to the medium than I was, interpreted thus—

"She says, '*Why did you not come to me on Sunday night? I wanted you to lift me in bed.*'"

Minnie gave her surname as well as this, which was not her Christian name, but a pet name by which she had been known. I am quite sure not a person in that room had heard one or the other, or knew such a person ever existed. They were quite out of the circle of my everyday life. The medium had only just set foot in the Old World, and the séance was held at the opposite end of London from where Minnie lay dead. Not one of those present lived anywhere in the neighbourhood.

Whence came those whispered words? I cannot answer the question any better now than I could when they were uttered, and that is a good many years ago now.

Let me add another "parochial" experience.

It is evident that my sermons must have had an "occult" tone about them at this time; for people used often to come to me in the vestry after service, or write to me at home, on the assumption that I knew something of the Modern Mystery. No wonder that good Mrs. Grundy was scandalised!

A woebegone man came one day when I had just finished a series of sermons on "The

Future that Awaits Us." His wife had heard one or two, but she was in consumption, and had suddenly taken a turn for the worse. Would I come and see her?

He lived out of the parish, and simply gave me a card bearing the name of "Williams." He was a poor, feckless creature, worn out with sorrow and watching; but he was urgent that I should come, so I cast parochial etiquette to the winds and went. I began to feel that all the hanky-panky people belonged to my parish.

It was as I thought. Mrs. Williams had been a "follower" of mine because she felt I knew something of this added light as to the future—that I held some possible clue to the solution of the Great Secret. She thought I must have noticed her; but ours was a large church, with a crowded congregation, and I had not done so. The title of the series of sermons had caused her to go out when she ought to have been at home; it was, by the way, an Advent series; and now—well, now she was going to solve the secret for herself.

She had one strong wish, however, and it was a strange one too. She wanted to communicate with me directly she had crossed the bourn—to "come back" and tell me whether my speculations were true. Would I give her the chance? Would I exercise all my will-power to meet her half-way, as it were?

Of course I acceded to her request. It was just what I wished, though I should not have dared to ask it of a dying person. But here the dying person asked it of me.

It was literally so. I was present when the end came. Her little child was brought by her mother to bid her farewell. Her husband was prostrate; and then, when all seemed over, she pressed my hand quite perceptibly, and whispered in my ear as I bent over her, "*I will come.*"

I went straight from the deathbed, and told my wife to take pencil in hand and write;

when the following words came without any question being put :—

"The spirit you seek is with you."

"Your name?"

The married name was given; and I asked the maiden name. Now I did not know this; but I guessed. Sometimes when I had waited a short while in the drawing-room, I had taken up a book and found the name of "Hamilton" on the fly-leaf. I had jumped to the conclusion that the book belonged to Mrs. Williams before her marriage. Some name was written, I forget what now, but not Hamilton. The mother's name too I fancied was Hamilton, and I said so. The answer came rapidly written—"Stepmother."

Then I questioned her as to her little boy, whom I fancied they called Milton—perhaps Hamilton again. What was his Christian name?

"Willie."

"But they called him Hamilton or Milton when they brought him to your bedside, did they not?"

"Yes. Pet name."

And so on. Question after question was answered with amazing rapidity—amazing dexterity, I ought to say—for every reply was utterly false, as I found afterwards from Mr. Williams. The mother's name *was* Hamilton, as was Mrs. Williams' before marriage, and the child bore the name of Hamilton too, as a Christian name. The ingenuity with which these and other questions were fenced was remarkable.

And such "staggerers" were far from rare. At one time I used to have a little séance of three or four serious inquirers at home on a Sunday evening after service. I thought we might be in a good frame of mind then. One night nobody seemed to be coming; but at last, quite late, a friend of mine—a barrister, who would probably visit me with all the terrors of the law if I hinted at his personality—put in an appearance. We usually sat at a small chess-table; but I had not cleared this, as nobody seemed coming. It had rather a strange occupant. I suffered just then from a mania for keeping snakes, and had picked up a splendid specimen of a hedge-snake at the Covent Garden Conservatory the day before. As I had no cage, I turned up my waste-basket on the chess-table, and kept the reptile there. I was somewhat at a loss what to do with it. My legal friend was a writing medium, and he solved the difficulty for me by writing—

"*Put him in the cupboard. Hurry up, and put the d——d old serpent in the cupboard.*"

I insert that expletive because it was characteristic. Neither my friend nor myself garnish our speech with those ornaments; but every communication that evening was full of oaths. We were told on the next occasion that the communicating intelligence was a departed bargee. He certainly swore like one; but this experience only happened on one single occasion.

Not this—but worse!

On another of those Sunday evenings there were present the barrister, who had brought us *en rapport* with the bargee, and the French gentleman, who habitually announced that he was attended by a certain undesirable personage. The announcement was repeated on this occasion, and somebody—probably the bargee-barrister—suggested, "Why not sit for the devil?"

It was literally a case of the *advocatus diaboli;* but the proposal met with acceptance, and his Satanic majesty promised to put in an appearance, only we must go into a darker room than my study, where we were then sitting. It faced the street, and a glimmer of light sometimes entered even when the curtains were drawn; so we shouldered the chess-table, and adjourned to the schoolroom, where the darkness was Egyptian.

Our *diablerie* was simple enough. We just sat in the usual manner and reminded our unseen friend of his recent promise, when in an instant the table rose violently under our hands and was as violently dashed on its legs again, *so* violently that the frail article was smashed into several fragments. We gathered up the débris, and retreated without waiting for further developments. I wonder whether we were just a little frightened without either of the three caring to confess it? At all events, we made the absence of a table the excuse for not opening up communications; though another might have been found without going very far, if we had been particularly anxious about it.

As an example of practical diabolism, this incident is just a little feeble. To make it piquant, the intelligence should have supplied the absence of a table by his own personal presence; but the plain fact was, he did not get a chance, unless he had been very brisk indeed. For some reason or other, "the dauntless three" retreated from that school-room in double-quick time, carrying with them the relics of their Delphian table.

This, as I have said, was the only instance

of *diablerie* pure and simple in which I ever took joint action with others. My few and far-between excursions into the grim and dangerous realms of black magic have been, by the necessity of the conditions, made alone and in the dead of night.

But there is one incident to which we have always given the name of "The Witches' Kitchen," of a character which, I am sure, would have earned Mrs. Grundy's warmest anathema, had she been "there to see." When I availed myself of the offer made by Miss Nicholl—afterwards Mrs. Guppy and then Mrs. Volckman—to give me a séance at my own house, I invited no one else to be present. I did not know whether she would care for visitors, they might spoil "business;" and moreover I did not, on my own account, care to risk a fiasco before others.

On this first occasion Miss Nicholl, my wife, and myself sat in my study, and scarcely any manifestations occurred. The only one

I can recollect was curious enough, but not very much to the point. I was just then, be it recollected, trying to establish the fact of "spirit-identity." I accepted the phenomena, and favoured the pneumatological theory; but were the intelligences those of our own kith and kin, who had passed on— "not lost but gone before"?

Under my study table, at which we were sitting, was a violin in its case, and on this latter my feet were resting as on a footstool. Suddenly the strings of the violin—inside the closed case, recollect — were violently twanged several times as though some unseen executant were performing a *pizzicato* passage, which was neither harmonious nor melodious, but exceedingly puzzling, considering that my feet still reposed on the outside of the lid.

The reason which Miss Nicholl gave my wife in private for the paucity of results that evening was remarkable too, but not of a nature which I can set down here. She offered to come again, saying she would bring a friend with her, Mrs. Sims, the sister of Mr. Alfred Russel Wallace; and she asked us to invite one or two sympathetic inquirers. The circle would, she thought, be sufficiently large then. Our choice fell on Mrs. Turner, the wife of a clergyman then officiating at Berkeley Chapel, Mayfair, and Miss Houghton, who was famous as a producer of "spirit-drawings."

After we had sat some time, Miss Nicholl grew very uneasy, saying there was a collision of opposite forces. She more than hinted that my wife's "guides" and her own were not sympathetic. Soon after, all our chairs, which were heavy high-backed ones, began to rock violently, while we all experienced the sensation that the room itself was being shaken, as I had often felt when sitting with Home. So far the experience was a pretty good representation of a miniature earthquake, or the saloon of a Channel steamer during a lively passage. Then Mrs. Sims declared that she was seized by the throat, and she looked as though such were the case. Miss Houghton rose to "demesmerise" Mrs. Sims; and this broke the charm, for up to this time we had all been rocked backwards and forwards in our chairs. My wife and Mrs. Turner became frightened, and honestly declaring they had "had enough of it," left the room. Miss Houghton was still engaged in her demesmerisation, and Miss Nicholl was sitting in a half-dazed condition. My own attention was particularly directed to an article of furniture in one corner of the room, which continued to sway backwards and forwards after the chairs had become quiescent. It was a "whatnot," covered with china ornaments, none of which were thrown down, as in the ordinary course of gravitation they ought to have been. I was particularly interested in the evolutions of this chattel, and, as I had nothing else to do, I walked up close to it and watched it sway idiotically backwards and forwards until it gradually subsided. At the same time Mrs. Sims "came to," and Miss Nicholl grew tranquil. The two scared sitters came back, and we went serenely to supper.

The questions remained, however—and they remain still—How came those chairs to be rocked, and that article of furniture to oscillate?

It is no use for the scientist to say, as Sir David Brewster did about the table, that "it *appeared* to move." It did move. I was as calm and collected then as I am now, years and years after, when I write these words; and if I am to trust my eyesight in any of the ordinary concerns of life, that "whatnot" swung like a pendulum for several minutes. Everything, I should observe, in this Witches' Kitchen experience, occurred in the full light of three gas-burners and in my own drawing-room, where, of course, anything like collusion or preparation was quite impossible. I have no idea as to the rationale of it all. I only know the incidents occurred just as I have set them down, and I am afraid it would be useless for the greatest savant under the sun to tell me I must distrust my ordinary senses in deference to the dogma of common sense as to what *ought* to have happened. Common sense was clearly in abeyance for the time being, and I know I had my wits about me. In fact, my only anxiety was lest the noise of the swaying chairs should attract some of the servants, and I carefully secured the door when the two scared sitters had departed, as I did not know what developments might be in store for us.

No doubt Mrs. Grundy would join the Catholic Church on one side, and the scientists on the other, in putting a veto on such proceedings as those of the Witches' Kitchen. The combination is curious, but respectable. What one fails to see is how the Church, as by law established, and the chapels, can lay the same embargo on free inquiry.

I fear, however, the adherents of church, kirk, or chapel, would have seen little with which they would have cared to claim kinship in the decidedly uncanny proceedings of our Witches' Kitchen.

CHAPTER VIII

STUDYING THE STARS

" A sad astrology, the boundless plan
That makes you tyrants in your iron skies,
Innumerable, pitiless, passionless eyes,
Cold fires, yet with power to burn and brand
His nothingness into man."
—TENNYSON, *Maud*.

WHEN describing my own passage through the hands of the Masters, I took occasion to mention that Mr. Hockley tried his best to initiate me into the doctrines of astrology, and that I had proved an inapt pupil. Of all the multiform branches into which that comprehensive subject called occultism breaks up, this appears to me the one which most imperatively demands special faculties on the part of the professor. The astrologer, like the poet, is born, not made.

But again, I was fortunate in the homely

aspects of my occult study. My wife proved as apt a student as I myself was the contrary; and I could quite accept the doctrine once laid down by my unseen guides, when they said that these special gifts were given to her for my benefit, because she was the only one in whom I should believe. I am, in fact, a stiff-necked and stubborn sceptic, though I daresay some of my readers will not give me credit for it. But the most thorough-going unbeliever will probably draw the line at his own domestic threshold, especially when the partner of his existence, as in my case, does not try to force her doctrines down his throat, or parade her gifts before him for his discomfiture.

Without the special advantages which I had in the way of instruction, my wife took up the study of astrology on her own account, and it came to her quite naturally. That is exactly the expression—"it came naturally"—as I hold all intellectual gifts should come; they are not gifts if they have to be forced. They may be cultivated, but the faculty must be there first. You may develop musical gifts to any extent, but nothing will give a man an ear for music if nature has left him lacking in that respect.

My first astrological experiences were gathered from a professor named Wilson, who lived in the Caledonian Road. Hitherto I have carefully veiled his identity when writing about him, because the poor man was a good deal persecuted during his lifetime; but, like so many of whom I have had occasion to speak, he has gone over to the majority, and is no longer liable to be prosecuted as a rogue and a vagabond because he received a modest half-crown fee for the exercise of his "spiritual gifts."

I had been consulting Mr. Hockley on some matter—I forget what—and he had given his reading of the figure he had erected according to the date I had given him for my birth; but there was some little uncertainty about the exact hour and minute of my nativity, and he thought he would like a second opinion. I proposed we should go together to Wilson, who lived close to Mr. Hockley's abode. "You can give me a nod," I said, "if the man knows his business. If he is a mere charlatan, there is no need to waste time with him."

We went, and consulted the wizard in his little unpretentious back parlour. He was even then old, but after the two astrologers had exchanged a few words, which were only partially intelligible to me in my condition of heathen darkness, the expected nod came. Wilson was all right, and Mr. Hockley left me to my *tête-à-tête* with him, saying he had only come to introduce me.

Then the old man tried back, and, by checking the events of past life, fixed upon one of the epochs I had named as the alternative day and hour of my birth. It came so close upon midnight as to render the uncertainty important.

There was the past mapped out before me

like a chart; and the old man said he would keep the figure in his book ready for use at any future time, if I wished to consult him. Without saying of him that he told me all things ever I did, he told me quite enough to make it clear that we had got the right date, and that there was "something in" astrology.

Amongst all the various forms of occultism surely this is the one to which that self-stultifying word "supernatural" is least applicable. If the sun and moon sway the tides, why should they leave man untouched? If the testimony of language be worth anything, Greek, Latin, and English bear evidence that the "moon-struck" owe their infirmity to the evil influence of our satellite. But it is not my present purpose to argue about theories or refer to other people's experiences. What I have to do is to give such passages of my own personal history as appear to establish the fact that "the stars in their courses" do affect our destinies, and that it is possible for gifted persons to read those destinies not only as fulfilled in the past, but as lying stored up for us in the future.

I shall be inartistic enough, then, to give an instance of this in my own experience, which is quite as remarkable as any of which I have ever read in tale or history. Of course, according to artistic rules this episode ought to be reserved as a *bonne bouche* until the last, but I give it here at the outset, if only to guard against the supposition of being moon-struck myself. I can see no explanation of the facts short of believing that astrology is just as much a fixed science as astronomy.

Fortunately I am able in this instance to give names in full, so that my narrative may be checked if necessary.

The astrologer who figures in this case is Mr. T. L. Henly, a gentleman who has made it his mission in life to develop the cultivation of flax as a home industry, and who has taken out several patents for the treatment of that fibre. But, like the Swedish seer, Swedenborg, Mr. Henly combines with this practical and material pursuit a strong taste for occultism. He is, at the time I write, living and working successfully, so that he can "witness if I lie." He had been dining with me one Sunday, and went to "sit under" me in the evening at a parish church in the suburbs where I was Sunday evening lecturer.

As we were walking to church he said, "I have been looking over your horoscope, and I find there is a windfall coming to you in a month's time."

I told him I was extremely glad to hear it, and naturally inquired whether he could inform me how this particular windfall was to come.

Yes, he said; it would be occasioned by a death.

I cast about, and said there was only one person in existence whose death would be likely to benefit me. Could he be alluding to the "unexpected death" of this "old lady"?

No, it was not a lady. It was a gentleman whose death would do me good. The death, he said, would be the result of an accident. "And moreover," he added, "it is a death which will be talked of from one end of England to the other."

I quite failed to guess who my illustrious friend or relative could be, and concluded in my omniscience that he was talking at random. We changed the subject. I preached my sermon, and soon forgot all about the prognostication.

A month from the date on which this prophecy had been uttered was Whitsunday.

I was still combining journalistic work with my clerical and scholastic duties; and just then I used to write four leaders each week for Mr. Edward Spender, who was editor of the National Press Agency in Shoe Lane, and also London editor and part proprietor of the *Western Morning News*.

Every now and again Mr. Spender used to go to Plymouth for the purpose of auditing the accounts of his journal, and on those occasions I had to fill his chair at the National Press Agency.

On the day succeeding the Whitsunday I went down to the office, as Mr. Spender was then absent on one of his accustomed expeditions to the west of England, when I found on my desk a telegram containing the following words :—

"*Mr. Spender and his two sons were drowned yesterday at Plymouth.*"

Then I remembered the prophecy of a month back, and felt how false the prediction was. Instead of being a windfall, this event had put a sudden stop to work which had been pleasant, and, in my modest estimation, fairly remunerative.

It was quite true that the death was talked of from one end of England to the other. It was, in journalistic language, "startling." The father and two sons were bathing in

Whitsand Bay, when a tidal wave came and swept them off. The event is commemorated in a monument which stands on the shores of the bay.

But a windfall to me! How could that be? Well, it was so after all; for, quite contrary to my expectation, I succeeded to Mr. Spender's editorship, and retained it for several years, until I vacated it for another appointment.

The prophecy, therefore, was correct in every detail, and, as I have said, it was given to me a full month before its fulfilment exactly as I have here reported it.

I am quite at a loss to guess what "explanation" could be given of these facts, save that the coming event had cast its shadow before, and that Mr. Henly read that event in my horoscope as in a book.

I need scarcely add, since it will have been apparent on the face of my narrative, that there was no "professional" element in all this. Not only did Mr. Henly give his prophecy without fee or reward, but he also added such instructions to my wife as to enable her to develop her gift; and I am thus fortunate in possessing a sibylline oracle under my own roof.

No later than last year this sibylline oracle turned out a curiously correct response. Years before, the sibyl predicted that in 1894 there would be a little legacy for us, though she had the best reason for knowing that nobody was likely to make us a bequest. But in 1893, surely enough, the unexpected death of an old lady did occur, and the bequest came in due course in the year following, for the executors took pretty nearly the full allowance of a year and a day for winding up the estate, and thus unconsciously confirmed "the stars in their courses." There had been estrangement between myself and that old lady, and the probabilities of my inheriting under her will were more than remote. But peace to her ashes! The old lady in question forgot her grievance, so that she in her turn added her quota of confirmation, too, to the truth of occultism. She would scarcely rest in her grave if she knew she had done so.

But I did not, for all this, neglect my little shrine in the back parlour down the Caledonian Road. I liked to check one oracle by the other—Delphi by Dodona. I had been absent from London for a time, and had got out of the groove for literary work in consequence. I wanted to get back again, and asked Wilson whether I could do so. Yes, he replied, but not until next July—which was then a long way off. Then, he said, there was an aspect of Mercury which portended success in something connected with literature. I must wait. I waited; and in July two editorships were offered to me. I was in the position of Captain Macheath, but I made my choice, and retained my post for six years, when the journal I edited passed into other hands.

During my absence from London I had been helped in my work by the husband of my eldest daughter, and I left him as my successor when I returned to town. He was successful; but I wanted them back, and went to Wilson, telling him just so much. I wanted my daughter to come back to London, but I did not wish her husband to return until I could put him in some position as good as that he was leaving. "Let them come," he said; "there will be a post open for him. Indeed," he added, "it will be waiting for him when he gets here." This was literally true. Before he had completed his arrangements for return, a post fell vacant in my old office, and it required some management on my part to keep it open for him until he came back; but I succeeded, and he retains that post still.

Surely the cases I have cited might go some way towards answering the question as to the *cui bono* of occultism.

As I am not ambitious of writing a folio, I must content myself with these specimens of astrology proper, which, it will be seen, are happily free from that vagueness which too often accompanies oracular responses. In fact, I must in justice say that I have never met in this branch of the occult with anything analogous to the

"*Aio te, Aeacida, Romanos vincere posse*"

of the old historic oracle.

As the physical configuration is, rightly or wrongly, attributed to planetary influence, I shall take leave to include palmistry and physiognomy in my "Study of the Stars." The following is the diagnosis of my character and fortunes from the study of my hand. It was given by Mrs. Louise Cotton, a lady who, like so many of the rest, has gone over to the majority. She had just begun to make a name in the science of Desbarrolles when she died at a comparatively early age. The delineation is valuable not so much intrinsically, because my readers cannot check its correctness, nor can I with due modesty claim possession of that highest of all gifts, self-knowledge, as to satisfy them on this point. I append it in full, however, because I think it is extrinsically important, as showing the lines upon which the professors of palmistry work. After devoting some two hours to the examination of my hands under a powerful magnifying-glass in the pretty consulting-room of her house in Abingdon Villas, Kensington, Mrs. Cotton sent, in due course, the following exhaustive

Delineation.

"The fingers of these hands are conical, a modification of the psychic or pointed type, the general characteristics of which are love of beauty, artistic instincts, inspiration, and great impressionability. But as this subject is gifted with a large thumb and a medium development of the joints (of order and the philosophic), his instincts expand themselves logically, modifying in a great measure the pronounced qualities of the conic hand. He will be subject to sudden changes of temperament, and will dislike anything like tyranny either in politics or religion, which might be liable to drive him into extremes. He has the instinct of order so far that he likes to have things in their places, though he may scatter them the next moment, and he will prefer that others should carry out for him the order and regularity which he appreciates so much. He is ambitious, has artistic tastes, and will be likely to cultivate either music or painting. He is a little fond of speculation, but will never be very lucky. The rather long fourth finger indicates a love of reading and acquiring knowledge. He likes to know 'the reason why' of most things; is a little argumentative; will accept nothing without examining it by the light of reason, and has his own ideas on most subjects. He has a great taste for detail, and is very observant of little things. He will be apt to worry himself extremely over trifles; and yet the same fondness for detail will often have been useful to him through life. He is very active and energetic, though he thoroughly appreciates ease and comfort. He is extremely sensitive, and easily wounded by fancied slights. The thumb, containing the chief motor powers of life, is a large one; the second phalanx (logic) being excessive in size, showing excellent reasoning powers. The first phalanx (will) is smaller, therefore he is not always able to act according to the suggestions of his better judgment; and it is possible he may be easily led or persuaded to act sometimes against it; but he can be obstinate in some things, and has a hasty, irritable temper, with much penetration.

"The planets (known by the 'Mounts,' &c.) which exercise chief influence over his life are Jupiter, Saturn, the Moon, and Mercury, with Venus and Mars secondary. Jupiter endows him with an impetuous temper and much intelligence. It would indicate great success and distinction in life by the

Star on the Mount of Jupiter and other signs; but the transverse lines, which are also there leaning to the malefic planet Saturn, also the latter's mount and line (as well as that of the Sun) being *cut* by the 'Girdle of Venus,' all denote many hindrances and obstacles throughout the career, and show that the good fortune which may come does not last. Saturn adds much nervous impressibility, and, in combination with Mercury and the Moon, a love of and intuition in occult sciences. The Moon gives him imagination and a little caprice. The Sun and Mercury add bright intelligence, chiefly by deduction. The latter planet gives finesse, love of science, eloquence, &c. Venus endows him with a warm, sensuous temperament, an ardent nature, melody in music, and many amiable qualities. Mars adds the force of resistance more than aggression.

"The *Line of Life* shows illness at the age of twelve, also at twenty-four; the health out of order about twenty-seven or twenty-eight and about thirty-one; at forty, illness, with delicacy lasting some time after; health again affected at forty-seven, fifty-four or fifty-five, sixty or sixty-one, but the life will reach seventy.

"The *Line of Head* shows caution, good brain power, and, in combination with the large phalanx of logic, excessive reason, carefulness, and calculation. The dark spot on this line indicates suffering in the head, either headaches, earache, or the eyes affected. The union of the three vital lines implies danger to the life, probably through an accident, in early life.

"The *Line of Heart* is very long, indicating excessive affection, and shows some disappointments in friendship, and trust betrayed. The Girdle of Venus being present, adds force and energy to the passions; but, as it opens out on the Mount of Mercury, it indicates that they have found a safer channel to exhaust themselves than through the sensual instincts.

"The *Line of Fate*, beginning in the Mount of the Moon, denotes that much of the happiness or unhappiness of this subject comes through others. There is a loss of money in the family early in life; a death at twenty-three or twenty-four; a woman's influence is in the fate at that time, and another at twenty-seven, ending in marriage, which has been fairly happy; but the line is very fluctuating, many changes and troubles being shown. Other deaths appear at twenty-eight or twenty-nine; a great change about fifty, and changes about fifty-five or fifty-seven. The line is smoother in later life.

"The *Line of the Sun*, or Fortune, is broken in many places, showing that both money and position have been assailed from time to time. Occasionally there has been good fortune, but not lasting, a great destiny having been much spoiled by the bad influences of the planet Saturn. The end of life promises to be more peaceful and less unsettled.

"The *Line of Health* shows a liability to

throat affections. The 'gout line' is present, showing that either this disease or rheumatism is in the system.

"Some travelling and sea-voyages are indicated.

"The more fortunate days might be Monday and Thursday.   LOUISE COTTON."

I am generally credited by occultists with anything but the logical faculty here attributed to me, when I urge that the inevitable outcome of a full belief in astrology must be fatalism pure and simple. If you are "built that way," and the stars in their courses map out a certain course for you, that course you must follow, and what becomes of free will?

"No," replies the astrologer; "you are only warned. You can avoid the danger if you accept the warning; but you will suffer if you neglect it."

Surely that does not cover the case. Take that striking Whitsunday incident I gave at the beginning of this chapter. If I had guessed the meaning of the prediction, warned my friend, and kept him from going west, or from taking that sea-bath, where would have been the record of the stars? I can see no deduction short of purely pagan "necessity" if astrology stands good. With this deduction, however, I am glad to think I have nothing to do at present. I am giving facts, and the doctrines must take care of themselves; but I fail to see that I am illogical when I hold that the acceptance of astrology lands us in fatalism. I am only anxious to keep up the credit of my logical thumb.

CHAPTER IX

FROM SPIRIT TO MATTER

> " I am not dead,
> But in the body still; for I possess
> A sort of confidence, which clings to me;
> That each particular organ holds its place
> As heretofore, combining with the rest
> Into one symmetry, that wraps me round
> And makes me man."
> —NEWMAN, *Dream of Gerontius.*

MENTION has already been made of Mrs. De Morgan's book "From Matter to Spirit," for which her husband, Professor De Morgan, wrote the preface. That title was one very suggestive of the evolution of the indwelling spirit from its material surroundings; but the reversal of that phraseology describes the order of events which was observed in my study of occultism.

Let me very briefly recapitulate for the sake of clearness. First came the table-tilts and raps, non-intelligent in their earlier phase, but gradually linked with intelligence and made responsive to inarticulate questions. Then came such physical manifestations as sound of the "spirit-voice" and the touch of the "spirit-hand"—my inverted commas will show that I am using these expressions hypothetically, as quotations from the terminology of the occultists. Then came the apparition proper, where it was a clear case of *choses vues*, and the vision moreover was sensible to feeling as to sight. The gap between these earliest and latest phases, I need scarcely say, is immense.

And yet, curiously enough, I cannot recollect when it was I first saw an apparition at a séance. I am afraid I know the reason. I do not think I believed in the ghosts. I am not sure that I believe in them still; in fact, I am sure I do not believe in the large majority of them. There is a terrible Petticoat-lane, rag-and-bone-shop appearance about the average goblin of the séance-room, which demands a very capacious swallow indeed for acceptance. But, then, there are ghosts and ghosts. Some are quite above suspicion of being faked up. Is it not so in all society, material as well as "spiritual"?

The very earliest fragments of spirit-form which met my eyes were the hands which flitted about the cabinet of the Davenport brothers at an initial period of my career. Then there were some people named Holmes who gave a show in Quebec Street near the Marble Arch. They used to exhibit faces in a kind of Punch and Judy arrangement; only the dolls were not worthy of our national puppet-hero. They were more like the battered effigies of some Aunt Sally establishment. All these have to be cleared away as so much rubbish before one comes to the "spirit" faces and forms about the genuineness of which there could be any reasonable question.

Mrs. Guppy, the locomotive lady said to

have been wafted *à la* St. Cecilia from the northern heights of London to Mr. Williams's séance-room in Lamb's, Conduit Street, was formerly the photographer's assistant who had helped my French friend to his " Week with a Ghost," and she married as her second husband Mr. Volckman, one of the gentlemen who sat on the Committee of the Dialectical Society. She had séances for materialisation at her house in Notting Hill, when Mr. Williams used to retire into a cabinet, and, shortly afterwards, buccaneering John King would come round with a spirit-light and show his face to the assembled sitters. These were remarkable manifestations, for we were packed so closely into a small room that the place became like the Black Hole of Calcutta, and there was scarcely room to swing the proverbial cat, much less for that gallant corsair to go cruising about as he did.

Generally speaking, these spectral apparitions took place — like the spectrum for scientific analysis, let it not be forgotten — in blank darkness; but one day I received a notification from Mr. W. H. Harrison, then editor of the *Spiritualist*, that he had succeeded in producing the spirit-face in full light, and even in photographing it by the illumination of magnesium.

I set off at once to Hackney, where I found the medium for these spirits of light in a pretty little girl just emerging from her teens, and named Florence Cook. I sat at first with only the family party and Mr. Harrison, adjourning for the purpose to a room downstairs, which seemed a kind of housekeeper's apartment, with a cupboard in one corner. This had been converted into a cabinet, and had a hole cut at the top of the door for the face to show itself. In this cupboard stood a chair, and into that chair I fastened "Florrie," tying her as tightly as I could with tape, and sealing the knots. Then I closed the door, and was about to take my seat in the circle, or rather semi-circle, surrounding the cupboard; but as I was in the act of shutting the door, or the very instant I turned the handle, up came the face at the orifice.

Now, Florrie had a black silk dress on; and the figure, so far as I could see, had some white garment about the neck. Besides, even if it were possible that she could wriggle out of my knots—which I do not think she could—the rapidity with which she must have wriggled into them again was remarkable. I opened the door, and there was Florrie in the chair apparently entranced; so she must have got back as quickly as she got out of her integuments. It was very puzzling; and not the least part of the puzzle was that the face was very like Florrie's.

The "spirit" lips too were not voiceless, any more than Florrie's own were, and she prattled volubly. I was told I might touch the face, and I did, holding quite a long conversation at the peep-hole.

Later on in the series of séances—for I went to a good many—the full form came out of the cabinet, and walked about in our midst. Thereby hangs a tale.

It was whispered by the scandal-mongers —for scandal invades turning tables no less than tea-tables—that a sort of rivalry had grown up between the veteran Mrs. Volckman (if, indeed, it be not ungallant to speak of a lady as a veteran) and the rising little medium, Florrie Cook. It was, so said these chatterers Juno and Venus over again— *spretæque injuria formæ.* Without attaching the smallest credence to such idle talk, meeting it, in fact, with the pertinent inquiry of the context—

"Can heavenly minds such high resentments feel?"

it is still necessary to mention the report, because it was supposed to give a sort of key to what follows.

When the "form" emerged from the corner cupboard and came into our midst, it did so at first timidly and with much hesitation. "With a slow and noiseless footstep came that messenger;" but one little fact always formed a stumbling-block in the way of my perhaps hypercritical judgment, namely, there *was* a very distinct and palpable "footstep," though it was slow and noiseless. Florrie's double, that is, did not glide. It did not assume even the sliding gait of an average ghost in "Hamlet." It *walked*. I am fond of walking; but I own I had formed a sort of gratuitous axiom in my own mind that when, in the sweet by-and-by, I should expatiate in the asphodel meadows, I should "glide," instead of pacing them step by step as I had done the Surrey Hills or the Sussex Downs. Florrie's duplicate, as I have observed, "footed it" most unmistakeably.

Gradually the "messenger" grew more confident and came well up to us; but we were warned on no account to touch the figure, as by so doing we might work incalculable mischief to the medium who was presumably incarcerated in the corner cupboard. We obeyed implicitly.

But one night somebody did not obey. He broke the rules all to pieces by seizing the form and detaining it in his strong grasp. That "somebody" was Mr. Volckman.

There was, of course, a severe struggle, and a scene of wild confusion ensued, during which the figure retreated to its habitat in the cupboard, where afterwards Florrie was found in due course, and with no signs of a struggle apparent upon her person.

Now, when it is remembered that Mr. Volckman was a strong, vigorous man, and Florrie's double was as *bijou* as Florrie herself, most of us felt that the ghost on this occasion scored one.

Of course, it would have been more satisfactory if there had been *no* struggle—if the double had quietly disintegrated or vanished into thin air. But then, as I was constantly reminded in these investigations, we cannot manufacture our conditions. We must take them as they come, and explain them as best we may. I do not pretend to be a Hercules, but I felt then, and feel still, that if I had screwed my courage to the sticking place so far as to seize a small girl— assuming that it *was* a girl—I would have held her fast. The presumption, therefore, seemed to be that it was not a girl but a ghost, though, withal, a substantial one.

That substantiality was a constant *crux*. The patchwork appearance was a trial; but the solidity was staggering.

It is not, of course, for us to say what degrees of ethereality may lie between spirit and matter; but the trouble was, there seemed to be nothing at all ethereal in these visitants. John King's hand was just as firm, and gave quite as severe a grip as that bold buccaneer himself could have done "when clothed in clay." Was it possible that the impalpable spirit could have evolved such material integuments from the emanations of our bodies as we sat in circle? That was the theory.

Once at the Holmes's I had expressed a

desire to see my deceased brother, who was supposed to have "given in" to the spirits at the eleventh hour. They showed me a face; but it did not convince me. Then I was told there were difficulties, but if I would go forward into the darkness other signs should be given me which would be quite as satisfactory as the visible features. I went forward, and my hand was grasped by another hand which was quite large enough and sufficiently long to have belonged to my brother, who, by the way, stood some six feet three, and had grown very emaciated in his last illness. But still there might have been any number of tall spare people about in spiritland. I was not happy, and I told him so squarely; it is astonishing how familiarly, almost disrespectfully, one gets to speak to "spirits."

"My dear fellow," I said, "you must perceive my difficulty. I want to be sure it is you yourself, and a mere grasp of the hand is not sufficient to guarantee identity. Can you not say or do something that will put your personality beyond reach of reasonable doubt?"

He did not say anything in response, but he did something. He gave me a smart slap on the back. This, it is true, had been a way with him. He liked to come up behind you and attract your attention in this vigorous manner; but still the act was far too insignificant to serve as a mode of recognition.

On the whole, I feel that these apparitions, so-called, have been the least satisfactory of all the forms in which the Modern Mystery has presented itself to me. I am speaking, be it remembered, of my own personal experiences. If I were to fall back on testimony at second hand, this would be the most copious, instead of the most meagre, part of my narrative. But I am stiff-necked and sceptical, and am free to confess that in this department so enormous is the strain made upon belief that scarcely any evidence suffices to produce conviction. Even when I have "seen" myself—supposing the quasi-apparitions not to be of the rag-bag order—I rub my eyes and find myself asking what I had for dinner or supper as the case might be.

The most satisfactory piece of evidence—to me, that is—under this head is furnished in the following narrative, which can scarcely be deemed even one degree removed from being personal, seeing that it happened to my wife, who is far more pachydermatous than myself in these matters.

Some years after we had lost our boy, she was going upstairs one night when she saw our bedroom door standing ajar and a little face peering out at her as she approached. She concluded it was that of one of our other boys, and that he was playing tricks, as was not unfrequently the case, for the lad slept in a room adjoining our own and on the same floor as the boys' dormitory, where bolstering-matches and other irregularities used constantly to occur.

"Now, Bobby, I have caught you," said my

wife, and ran forward to suit the action to the word. Our room was empty, and Bobby was sleeping the sleep of innocence in his own crib. Then she remembered that the little head was curly as Johnny's had been, and as none of the others were; and she also recollected that this was a constant habit of Johnny to stand at a door and peep through before he came in. She declares to this day that she was not thinking of her dead child, nor had anything occurred to bring him specially to her recollection. Nothing came of the vision. It led to no result beyond itself; but you may as well try to shake her faith in the Thirty-nine Articles or the British Constitution as to make her doubt the fact that for one supreme moment she stood face to face with her departed boy.

Once, and only once, have I seen an apparition which I feel sure did *not* belong to the Petticoat-lane order. It appertains in order of events rather to the next chapter than this; but the subject is so germane to that on which I am now engaged, that I give the incident in detail here, and shall content myself with simply mentioning it in passing by-and-by. In this case both my wife and myself saw the apparition at the same time.

We had been witnessing some materialisations of—well, of a very materialistic order, and were both impressed with their unreality. It was then proposed that the medium should sit at the table, and endeavour to get materialisations there, instead of behind the curtains in the back drawing-room, where the show had been taking place. We sat in a pretty bright fire-light, myself on the medium's left, and my wife on his right. By-and-by there formed on the side where I was sitting, as if from the medium's side, a dwarfish figure, about the height of the table, but plainly the figure of a man — or a manikin. It seemed about the consistency of cigar-smoke — the proper attenuated form for a ghost to assume—

and disported itself for a while beside the medium, when it shambled right across the room, and finally disappeared behind the curtain separating the two rooms, and which had formed, so to say, the stage-drop for the previous performance. We both saw it distinctly for a considerable time, and an uncanny sight it was. Without being able to say why, I feel quite a qualm even now, at the distance of many years, when I write about it. But still it fulfilled one's idea of what a good attenuated ghost ought to be. I have had considerable experience in ghosts from Professor Pepper's downwards, and this one was decidedly the likeliest link between spirit and matter that ever came under my notice.

In more than one case I was promised that I should see the ghost and the medium together. That would of course have been very satisfactory. I did see it. That is, I saw the apparition emerge from its favourite back parlour and draw aside the curtains, showing what purported to be the recumbent form of the medium within. I saw this at Mrs. Fitzgerald's, in Cambridge Street, Hyde Park, when Williams was the medium, and again at the Cooks'; I mean, I saw a *something* recumbent in the darkness, which might have been Williams, or only Williams's discarded garments, and might have been Florrie Cook or—— This is how I put it to her.

"My dear girl, I have a great admiration for young ladies in their teens; but I know that they like to play their little tricks. I must see you more plainly than that, before I am convinced that it is my very friend Florence Cook."

She did not in the least mind these expressions of scepticism; and I am bound to say, both she and her sister Katie never refused any tests. On one occasion, besides tying Florence to her chair in the corner cupboard, I passed a long tress of her hair through a knot-hole in the cupboard door, and held that. There was the face, just the same as ever; and I am more than morally certain that Florrie did not wear a wig, for I pulled that tress with all my might and main, and tracked it down to its very roots.

Still it must be confessed that these manifestations constitute a very trying ordeal indeed; and I shall have something more to say about them in the succeeding chapter of my narration.

CHAPTER X

MYSTERIES IN MAYFAIR

"Sleep has its dreams, and life has its realities,
  The truth what is—or what appears to be—
Whether the oldest things are true vitalities;
  Whether we ought to believe in things we see;
Whether inquiry can find rest in theories Berkleyan,
Or if it be not worthiest, best, like the old Epicurean,
To think of nought but how to make the best of earthly
    trouble,
For all that seems substantial is an unsubstantial bubble.

But one thing certain is, whene'er we draw aside the curtain,
That nothing can befall us here but what is most uncertain.
As night from day and day from night, as evil turns to good,
And good to evil, wrong to right, in swift vicissitude—
As knowing most is but to know how little can be known;
As ere we see the moments here—the very hour is gone.
What can console us but the thought that out of dreams
    ideal
Imperishable work is wrought—the unchangeable Real?"
                                       —SIR JOHN BOWRING.

IN a little pill-box of a house which stood in Green Street, Grosvenor Square, lived at this time a lady who had every right to be called the high priestess of spiritualism.

This was Mrs. Makdougall Gregory, widow of Professor Gregory of Edinburgh. She has been dead for some years, and the *bijou* house at the corner of Park Street has given place to a stately red-brick block of flats. I cannot recollect how I first became acquainted with Mrs. Gregory; but she took me in hand very energetically, I suppose as being a "convertible" parson.

At Mrs. Gregory's, during a course of several years, I saw pretty well everything and everybody there was to see in connection with the Modern Mystery, and in its most pleasant form. The function of a séance in Green Street always assumed the form of an enjoyable dinner, where some seven people—rarely more—sat at a round table and talked of things which I often used to think must have made the footman's hair stand on end if he had not been old in his mistress's service, and therefore well seasoned in suprasensual subjects. There was generally a medium among the guests;

in fact I may say always, for the Rev. Stainton Moses was rarely absent. He was one of the masters at University College School, and for a long time the most intelligent advocate of the new doctrines. But the medium who was to officiate during the evening was almost always a guest too. We did not hurry the repast, for we were not afraid of running our deeds of darkness into the small hours of the morning. It was generally ten o'clock before we settled down to business.

I can, of course, only give a few particulars here and there of the remarkable things I saw and the notable people I met at these pleasant gatherings, which extended from first to last over a good many years.

All the mediums who came to London gravitated at once to Green Street, if they could get the entrée, and this was not difficult, for our hierophant—we want a feminine form for that word now—was anything but inaccessible.

Willie Eglinton was perhaps the medium

who had the longest "innings" at Green Street, always excepting, of course, Stainton Moses, who was more like a major-domo than a medium.

If a tithe of the wonderful events which occurred between Stainton Moses and his familiar "Imperator" had occurred to myself, I feel sure I should have been able to gulp down a whole Petticoat Lane of apparently faked-up ghosts.

I elected at the outset to give personal experience the preference over second-hand evidence however respectable; but Stainton Moses' testimony is *so* respectable, and he gave it to you in such a transparently sincere way over a cigar, that it could not fail to carry weight.

He was engaged a good deal with early English literature, and over and over again he would tell me how Imperator had given him page and line of a passage he wanted in Lydgate or some such author, which reference he would find, on consulting the edition at the British Museum, to be literally correct.

I daresay the following story has been published in one of Stainton Moses' numerous books; but I prefer to give it as I recollect hearing it from his own lips. The doing so seems to bring the narrative one degree nearer to being a personal one.

Stainton Moses was the last man to be dogmatic. He knew how necessary tests were for the unconverted, and he told Imperator one day straight out that he wanted an unquestionable proof that all these marvels in the way of reference and so on had not been elaborated by some specially exalted condition of his own inner consciousness.

Imperator mildly protested, but, in deference to the needs of weaker brethren, agreed to give Stainton Moses the test he required.

At the bidding of his familiar, my friend cleared out his writing-desk of everything but a sheet of paper and a pencil, locked the desk and placed it in a cupboard, which he also locked. Then he went out, locking the door of his room behind him.

When he returned he found a message written on the paper in this carefully guarded desk; and not only so, but, as if by way of taking a playful congé, Imperator had arranged all the toilet appliances, such as brushes, combs, and what not, in the form of a crop, on the bed.

It was curious at first to hear Stainton Moses talk of Imperator just as though the latter were an ordinary flesh-and-blood mortal. Of course, our modern transcendentalists always do this with regard to the "dear spirits," as they call them; but here was a man of far more than average intelligence adopting, not exactly the verbiage, but the same tone of conviction as any one of Professor Huxley's old women and curates in the hypothetical "cathedral town" could have done. It is difficult to guess why the sarcastic professor should have located his old ladies and curates in a *cathedral* town. Minor canons and *young* ladies would be more in keeping there; but that is, of course, a detail.

There was no hesitancy, no tone of scepticism or inquiry, about the tone of conversation in Green Street. We knew everything. We had settled it all. A general council could not have been more final than a squeaky assertion of "Peter," or "Joey," or some other of the many intelligences who haunted that little back drawing-room, especially when Eglinton or Williams happened to be ensconced behind the curtains.

One of the *most* final of all authorities was Gerald Massey, whom I had worshipped in my callow days as the author of "The Ballad of Babe Christabel," but whom I found so entirely different a person from what I expected to see when I met him in Mayfair. He always brought well to the front an Egyptian princess, from whom he got the information contained in his "Book of Beginnings," just as he went to the fountainhead for his information on the subject of Shakespeare's sonnets. The theory which, in this latter case, he derived from his intelligences, has stood the test of the severest criticism. It is, in fact, about the most rational account of the genesis of the sonnets, and it came entirely from "the other side"—I believe from the "dark lady" of the sonnets herself; but, in any case, when Gerald Massey buttonholed you, and brought his Egyptian princess to the front, you could not choose but hear, and you found it very difficult to doubt, such an intense tone of reality did the speaker throw into his words, and this air of reality was the very atmosphere of the little house in Mayfair. You stepped into Wonderland directly you crossed its threshold, much as Mr. Gladstone says you do when you pass into the domain of the Homeric poems from the commonplace things of ordinary existence.

At Mrs. Makdougall Gregory's I met Mrs.

De Morgan and her son. The occasion was the introduction of a raw-boned American girl, who possessed the gift of what is called psychometry in a remarkable degree. She would take a pebble in her hand, that is to say, and describe the geological conditions which surrounded it at its elaboration in pebble form. She would stop before an Egyptian figure, and describe in graphic language the scene under the particular Pharaoh from whom it dated. All this was wonderful; but unfortunately its correctness could not be checked. The following is a better case of psychometry, because, as will be seen, the accuracy of the vision could be properly appraised.

Mrs. De Morgan's son produced a ring, apparently belonging to a lady's finger, and said he believed she could say something about those to whom such articles had belonged.

"Yes," she replied, "spirits are often attracted to rings."

He asked her to examine this one and tell him what she saw.

She described an old grey-headed gentleman to whom the ring had belonged, and gave the minutest details of his personal appearance, adding that he seemed to her to be a foreigner.

I was sitting next to Mrs. De Morgan, and asked her whether this was the professor; but she said it was not.

When the ring was given back, the son told me it was one that an old French professor had presented to his father.

Now the curious point about this was that the questioner had purposely misled the medium. The ring, as I have said, was more fitted for a woman than a man; and when she said she could see the person to whom it had belonged, Mr. De Morgan said, "Will you tell me what *she* is like?"

"It is not a lady," she replied, "but a gentleman;" and then she went on to describe the old French professor.

Of course I questioned her about " my long-lost brother," simply asking her whether any spirit was present who took an interest in me.

"Yes," she answered, "there is a spirit present who is very anxious indeed to communicate with you—*so* anxious that he disturbs all conditions by his anxiety, and prevents the communication which he wants to bring about. He is tall — very tall — but looks so pale and emaciated. Do you recognise who it is?"

Of course I did, and told her so; but I could get no further identification.

It was here that the Rev. H. R. Haweis went through a great deal of the process of his "conversion." I was sitting one night with our hostess, Mr. and Mrs. Haweis, and Jesse Sheppard, the musical medium, who gives marvellous extemporisations on the pianoforte, and sings in all voices, from the shrillest of sopranos to the profoundest of basses. Mr. Sheppard, however, on that occasion was not exercising his musical but his ordinary mediumistic powers. The "spirits" always like the sitters to sing; and on this occasion they asked for melody. Strangely enough, though we had a musical medium present, no melody was forthcoming, and proceedings flagged. Our usual prima donna, Miss Katharine Poyntz, was not present.

"Come," said Mr. Haweis, "we can all of us sing a hymn. Will 'Jerusalem the Golden' do?"

The communicating intelligences signified their approval by vigorous raps, and we commenced. No sooner had we done so than a sharp smack was heard on the table, as though something had been thrown there. When the hymn was over we lighted up by direction, and found that the object laid on the table was a small mother-of-pearl cross with the word "Jerusalem" engraven on it in Hebrew letters.

Mr. Haweis has, as I remarked, borne frequent testimony in the pulpit to his belief in these revelations, and his utterances are on record in those deservedly popular volumes of sermons entitled " Thoughts for the Times" and "Speech in Season," which have run through goodness knows how many editions, and must be as gall and wormwood to episcopal critics. Mr. Haweis, for example, speaks of the priesthood as being " magnetic and spiritual ;" boldly asks the question, "Are the elements magnetised?" in the Communion, that is; and moreover explains the verbal inspiration of Scripture as being due to "automatic writing." The following extract from "Thoughts for the Times" affords a good specimen at once of Mr. Haweis's style, and of the line of thought pursued :—

"As of old, men crave for signs and wonders. They think they would believe if occasionally one rose from the dead. But what would be the use of that? If a flaming spirit descended at this moment into this church, bearing a revelation from the Invisible, don't you think we should have fifty explanations of the occurrence ready by tomorrow morning, and a facetious article upon the subject in the next *Saturday Review?* Is there one medical man present who, in spite of his own senses, would not be prepared to maintain the hallucination theory, rather than the supernatural theory?"

Another *habitué* of the little house in Mayfair, though not, I think, at the more esoteric gatherings, but only when a great gathering took place, was Philip James Bailey, the author of "Festus." My acquaintance with him, however, did not begin at Mrs. Gregory's, but was due to what looked at first like a bit of telepathy. I had been giving some lectures on poets, with musical illustrations from their works, and was sitting over my MS. of one on Bailey's "Festus," a poem I had admired from my boyhood, and felt I should like to know the author. As I wrote at my lecture, a servant entered my study and laid on my table a card, inscribed "Philip James Bailey."

It was no hocus-pocus, however, as I soon discovered when I asked him how he had found me out. He had called at the Free Public Library in the neighbourhood, he said, and, as his custom was, inquired whether they had Bailey's "Festus"—keeping his own identity concealed, but anxious to know how near he was to being a popular poet. They had a copy, the librarian told him, but, strange to say, it was then out, as it was in slight demand; then Bailey asked the name of the appreciative borrower, and so got my address.

A better instance still of a pseudo-ghost-story occurred during the Gregorian régime. One summer holiday I was taking the duty at Christ Church, Lancaster Gate. My family were at the seaside, and I used to run up on Saturday and return on the Monday morning. The magnetic governess kept house, and the talented organist of Christ Church, Mr Frederick Archer, used to come to lunch with me every Sunday. One day we sat down, the three of us—the governess, Archer, and myself — to a séance after luncheon. Little occurred, as our time was short, and I failed to get a note struck on the piano, though the communicating intelligence intimated its readiness to perform a solo to that extent. Archer went, and I retired for my afternoon nap. The governess nodded over a book, when suddenly there was a smart blow struck on one of the notes of the piano. The "spirits" had performed their promise then, and the governess was scared out of her wits. After evening service, I returned alone, and she was telling me of her experience. I asked her if she had not been dreaming, and she was assuring me such was not the case, when, lo, the note was struck again! It may be taken as an instance of my still indwelling scepticism, that I always liked to look into the natural courses of events before falling back on a "supernatural" theory. In a moment I had the front of that pianoforte off, and my ghost stood revealed. A mouse had made its way into the instrument at the back, nibbled the felt from the hammers, and out of that material had built itself a comfortable nest among the wires. The curious point of the business was that the creature should have so timed its ascent or descent as to twang the note when the governess was alone, and again when she was telling me her story. These are, of course, nothing more than "curious coincidences;" and I have a notion that if we set to work to collect these, we should get together almost as remarkable a mass of facts as in the realm of hanky-panky; and the best of it would be that nobody would credit us with lunacy for our pains.

Mrs. Makdougall Gregory's great mistake, as is generally the case with ardent propagandists, lay in the direction of *trop de zèle*. Instead of leading her neophytes gently through the earlier stages of the creed, she would take a hardened unbeliever, or a person who had never seen even a table twirl, and land such an one plump on one of Mr.

Eglinton's "materialisations," which usually assumed the following shape.

The little back drawing-room was divided from the larger one in front by a curtain, behind which Mr. Eglinton would retire for the purpose of being entranced. After a pause, of long or short duration as the case might be, the curtain would be drawn aside, and a ghost in Oriental attire, but looking as solid as Mr. Eglinton himself, would put in an appearance. His name was supposed to be "Abdallah;" and after he had submitted to our scrutiny for a while, the curtains would be drawn again; whilst, in due course of time, Mr. Eglinton would emerge in his dinner-dress, rubbing his eyes as though just waking from his trance.

I was present when Lord Rayleigh was brought suddenly face to face with this staggering apparition. Lord Amberley sat out some dinners and séances, but soon after expressed his opinions very freely in print on the subject of "spiritualism." Professor

Blackie was a frequent guest; and I have been present when Charles Bradlaugh and Dr. Kenealy went through the trying ordeal. The number of people with handles to their names would make my page like a column of the "Court Circular" if I transcribed them. "In sooth a goodly company!"

Our kind, but in this respect over-zealous, hostess was not quite easy about the genuineness of Abdallah herself; but she would not listen to my little plan for testing his authenticity. I offered to forego my dinner and quietly go to the drawing-room while the guests were circling the round table. Then I would get under the sofa in the back drawing-room, see everything that went on, wait until medium and guests were gone, and report progress to the hostess in private.

It was a self-denying scheme, on which I still look back with commendable pride; but it was declined with thanks.

"If you saw anything, I am sure you would not be able to remain still," said Mrs.

Gregory. I assured her I should, and bade her look hopefully at the other alternative.

"If I carried out my scheme, and saw nothing but what was genuine, what a magnificent testimonial it would be for the medium!"

It was, however, throwing words away. The good lady could not trust me; so we had to trust Abdallah as best we could.

It was after one of these Abdallah séances that the apparition of the manikin mentioned in the last chapter occurred.

Some people are disposed to believe that genuine apparitions *do* occasionally occur, but that they cannot be relied upon. The mediums cannot give results, and this, it is said, is where the Petticoat-lane business comes in. If I had to discount my own experiences in this liberal fashion, it would really amount to saying that I had only seen one case of what I felt to be genuine materialisation— that, namely, of the manikin; whilst all the rest might be "leather and prunella," though

I have no notion how the mediums work up those materials so cleverly as they do. That, of course—supposing them to be tricksters—is what they would call "biz." The explanation given by confirmed "spiritualists" when their favourite mediums are caught red-handed with elaborate costumes prepared for the occasion, always seemed to me a little far-fetched. They do it all unconsciously. It is the naughty spirits who make them do it. They don't mean any harm—it is almost pathetic to hear the apology of the hardened believer—they are only "elementals" and know no better, nor do they consider into what trouble they get the unfortunate medium by their little games.

Looking back through the vista of years on those many pleasant evenings spent in Mayfair, I cannot feel that I got much out of them in a psychical way, agreeable as they were physically.

They were rather like Lord Rayleigh's newly discovered constituent in our atmosphere—argon. They did not seem to blend with anything else, and they were to a large extent inoperative. "Society" manners and "spiritualism"—using both terms under protest—do not seem to harmonise.

A frequent experience of my own at the little pill-box in Mayfair seems the key to the whole position, though I did not see this at the time. Mrs. Makdougall Gregory liked to have me near her at the dark séance; I gave her vitality or magnetism. What with late hours and a good dinner, I used often to feel remarkably sleepy as soon as the lights were put out. She could feel me nod, or she would put a question to me and get no reply for a moment. Then I would blunder out an apology, which she always stopped by saying, "Don't apologise. It is not natural sleep. It's *magnetic*." The explanation came like a *deus ex machinâ* to solve my difficulty; and one cannot help sometimes wondering how much of the Modern Mystery is explicable by the easy theorising of its professors and some such simple solution as the mouse running up—not the clock—but the wires of the pianoforte keys.

Of course no such heretical idea ever found utterance on any tongue at the period of which I now write; though I am afraid I could not with truth say that these ideas never crossed my mind, especially when I was face to face with Abdallah. He and John King, the bold buccaneer, were terrible trials even for an advanced student of occultism.

CHAPTER XI

A MYSTIC ORATORY

"In the meditation of Divine mysteries keep thy heart humble and thy thoughts holy; let philosophy not be ashamed to be confuted, nor logic blush to be confounded: what thou canst not prove, approve; what thou canst not comprehend, believe; and what thou canst believe, admire; so shall thy ignorance be satisfied in thy faith, and thy doubts swallowed up with wonders. The best way to see daylight is to put out thy candle." —QUARLES.

> "The desire of the moth for the star,
> Of the night for the morrow;
> The devotion to something afar
> From the sphere of our sorrow."—SHELLEY.

I CAN quite believe it possible that a reader, even after patiently pursuing the course of my narrative to the present point, might still be inclined to ask in what particular this recital differs from the thousand and one that have preceded it.

Coming thus late in the day, it might fairly be demanded that this history should show some speciality to differentiate it from those that have gone before. True, it might be urged, you have given us some details that have not yet appeared, and you have shown us how those details affected you personally or dovetailed into your individual history; but more than one cleric has already told his story and given us so far a pleasing variation from the records of those who approached the subject in a quasi-scientific spirit. Have you anything to add which has not before been dealt with by your " cloth"? If so, what is it?

This I feel to be at once a fair demand, and also the one that I can answer most satisfactorily. The differentiating feature in my case is that I did not stop short at faith, but proceeded to practice.

In opposition to the occultists themselves who repudiated the idea that their system constituted a religion; in opposition more diametrical still to the orthodox, who held that occultism was irreligious, I felt almost from the first—certainly from an early stage of my occult studies—that occultism was either a religion, or it was, for me, nothing. I had no pretensions to scientific training, so I could not deal with the subject under that aspect. It soon became too serious a matter to be the mere plaything which many people make it. I accepted it as that which the judgment of Paris originally declared it to be, a demonstration of what had hitherto been mere matter of faith; and I felt that demonstration implied action. After mature thought, I came to the conclusion that the proper form which the system of occultism ought to assume in my hands would be an oratory service followed by a séance. The service and the sitting would, I thought, react one upon each other, and both gain in solemnity.

Accordingly I took two rooms over those occupied by the British National Association of Spiritualists in Great Russell Street (though the Association was, of course, in no way responsible for my proceedings), and fitted one up as an oratory, where I had a service twice a week, at which I officiated exactly as though I had been in church; and the service was immediately followed by a silent séance. I mean we did not indulge in the light conversation which generally prevails at those gatherings. I was still at that time engaged with regular duty in the Church of England, so neither of our services could be held on Sunday. They took place on Monday afternoon and on Thursday evening. The meeting on Monday was generally small, and I think we got the best results then. The numbers on Thursday evening were sometimes inconveniently large; but the sittings were by no means unprolific. I may give a single specimen of each.

One Monday afternoon Miss Katie Cook came to sit with us; indeed, she often did so on both days. Only five members were present, and we all joined hands, sitting at a round table and quietly awaiting manipulations, as our invariable custom was. This silence was only broken by the occasional singing of a hymn, our favourite one being that from Tennyson's " In Memoriam," which we set to the conventional tune for the " O Salutaris " :—

> " How pure at heart and sound in head,
>   With what divine affections bold,
>   Should be the man whose thought would hold
> An hour's communion with the dead.
>
> In vain shalt thou, or any, call
>   The spirits from their golden day,
>   Except, like them, thou too canst say,
> My spirit is at peace with all.
>
> They haunt the silence of the breast,
>   Imaginations calm and fair,
>   The memory like a cloudless air,
> The conscience as a sea at rest."

Miss Cook on this occasion wore a black silk dress, and she was sitting hand in hand with a member of the circle on each side. Presently a female form in white was seen gliding through the room. It advanced to a table behind me, on which stood a large cross covered with Balmain's luminous paint, and shedding a soft lambent light around. The figure stood on one side of this cross, and spread out its hand in front, so that we could see it quite distinctly. It then came behind me, put its hands on my head, and bending over, kissed me on the forehead. No word was spoken throughout the long period during which the figure passed from one to the other around the circle; and at the conclusion of the sitting Miss Cook was found as before, while the sitters on either side of her were quite sure that they had never for a moment loosened their hold. They had not held her by way of precaution or "test," but simply because it was our custom to sit thus.

One Thursday evening there was present in our circle a gentleman holding a high position on one of our daily papers, and his wife was presumably the medium on this occasion. Miss Houghton, a lady since deceased, became entranced, and the communication purported to come from a poor girl "with a past." She expressed herself as most thankful for the opportunity thus afforded of coming back to the scenes of her earthly life, and asked if she might kiss the hand of the medium who had enabled her to do so. The sitting ended with this; and when the light was brought, there was still a *wet tear-drop on the medium's hand!* Earlier in the evening, a lady had come late to the séance. The medium, who was exceedingly sensitive, shook convulsively, and said a poor drowned man was present and wished to communicate with the lady who had arrived late. She was the widow of a clergyman, formerly a brother curate of mine, who had gone out to Australia and was drowned with his two sons in a swollen river which he endeavoured to cross to take Sunday service at a church on the other side. She had only just arrived in England, and was a perfect stranger to the medium.

These oratory services were continued for

six months, and only ceased in consequence of my temporary removal from London.

When we resumed them, some time afterwards, we made the mistake of having a semi-public Sunday evening service in a hall, holding the private sitting afterwards in an adjoining room. The error was soon obvious. The spiritualists did not care to commit themselves to a strictly Church of England function; and the Church of England people thought the occultists necessarily wicked. It was a trial, and it failed, the services only being continued for two or three months in this place, after which we retired into privacy again.

The following was the announcement of the first month's services :—

SPECIAL SERVICES AND ADDRESSES ON SUNDAY EVENINGS.

The Addresses, on Subjects suggested by the "In Memoriam" of LORD TENNYSON, will be delivered as follows :—

I.—*Our Misnamed Dead.*
But trust that those we call the dead
Are breathers of an ampler day
For ever nobler ends.

II.—*The Enfranchised Spirit.*

Dare I say
No spirit ever brake the band
That stays him from the native land
Where first he walk'd when claspt in clay ?

III.—*An Hour's Communion with the Dead.*
How pure at heart and sound in head,
With what divine affections bold,
Should be the man whose thought would hold
An hour's communion with the dead !

IV.—*The Larger Hope.*
I stretch lame hands of faith, and grope
And gather dust and chaff, and call
To what I feel is Lord of all,
And faintly trust the larger hope.

The Service, based on the ancient "Missa Sicca," is one of Self-Dedication, Praise, and Commemoration of the Departed. It consists of passages from the Church of England Prayer-Book, and carefully selected portions of Hymns, Ancient and Modern. The order is as follows :—

1.—OPENING HYMN.
2.—LITANY OF THE HOLY SPIRIT.
3.—READING FROM "THE PERFECT WAY."
4.—SPECIAL HYMN OR ANTHEM.
5.—ADDRESS.
6.—OFFERTORY HYMN.
7.—SANCTUS.
8.—CONCLUDING HYMN.

It is of course at this point in my narrative I am most inclined to expatiate, and here too I feel the most urgent necessity for caution lest I become prolix and egotistical.

I cannot help assuming something like originality in my treatment of the subject at this period; and I still think that if it is to be utilised at all, it will be on these lines. No doubt, allowance must be made for what will be called "professional" prejudice on my part. I have no objection to the term, which need not be at all offensive. Nay, I have no doubt such considerations did weigh with me at the time of which I am treating; and I have, moreover, frankly acknowledged that they abide by me still.

It might appear that when I claim originality for my "ecclesiastical" treatment of these occult subjects, I am ignoring the prior claim of Mr. Haweis. I have already mentioned the outspoken way in which that popular preacher alluded to tabooed topics in his pulpit, and if I had to put the matter epigrammatically I would say that whereas Mr. Haweis was a Church of England clergyman first and a spiritualist afterwards, I reversed the process; I was a spiritualist first and a Church of England clergyman afterwards. He brought his occultism into church; I took my churchmanship out of church and located it, for the time being, in my mystic oratory.

At our penultimate semi-public service, when I had to announce my change of plan to my congregation, I had read as my lessons for the day (which I did not confine to Scripture) John Henry Newman's eloquent remarks on the ministry of angels, from his Oxford sermons, and another passage by Canon Liddon on "Concentric Circles of Adoration." This latter preacher was then recently dead, and I also quoted Canon Scott Holland's funeral sermon on the occasion, preached at St. Paul's Cathedral. All these men—the Cardinal and the two Canons—I claimed as Christian mystics, the former on the strength of the lessons I had just read, and Canon Scott Holland for the following eloquent passage in his funeral sermon on Canon Liddon:—

"He has passed into the hidden world, of which he ever gave us such glorious report, which was ever so nigh to him; and surely there he is even still bowing his knees before God the Father, and praying that those whom he has left on earth may be strengthened with the might of the Spirit. . . . That is still his prayer, and we can answer back. We can still remember him in our prayers before God; we who live in the same body of Christ of which he is still a member; who kneel before the same altar as that by which his life is still fed and his spirit purified. . . . Pray we for him, for his refreshment, for his illumination, for his eternal peace!"

Nay, I was eclectic enough to pass from church to chapel, from cathedral to conventicle, and quoted Dr. Clifford on the same subject. He said it was his habit to go to St. Paul's (for he was eclectic too) when Dr.

Liddon was preaching, as early as he could, so that he might get as near as possible to the speaker, "and so *feel the magnetism, the enthusiastic passion of the man.*" Were not the Cardinal, the Canons, and the Congregationalist minister himself here using the very language of the esoteric occultist?

Then followed details—paulo-post-future at the time—of my new scheme; and they were faithfully carried out for the best part of the year, so that I can speak of them in the past now. We are, however, now nearly up to date, and the whole thing is as clear before my own mind as though it happened yesterday.

A house happened to be on my hands in a quiet street of a sequestered western suburb. On the ground-floor was a fairly large double dining-room, which we fitted up plainly but appropriately as our chapel. We had our little altar on a footpace, vested in purple, and surmounted by a picture of the Madonna and Child. On one side was the organ, on the other the lectern, which served also for pulpit, and in a corner the circular table we used for our séances. Several dozen ecclesiastical chairs completed our modest arrangements, and we reserved this room entirely for services, at some of which a few specially invited outsiders might be present; but we no longer opened our doors to a public who had persistently refused to cross our threshold. We were promised exceptional results if we thus cloistered ourselves.

Upstairs was the séance-room proper, and a larger one for certain magical functions which were projected by one of our number. The other rooms were for the use of any members who wished to use them for private sittings, since each member had a key to the house, so as to come and go at pleasure.

It was really a very strange sensation to pass *out of the world,* so to say, leaving behind the little noises incidental to a "quiet" street in the suburbs of London, and coming into the region of perfect repose. One could not help feeling that such a scheme ought to succeed. We were definitely assured in the most solemn way that it should succeed, that our little oratory should be the frontier-line between the Seen and the Unseen, and that the Departed would come and join our simple worship—take the vacant places beside us, and lay their hands in ours. It was on this distinct assurance we set to work. Our regular functions were a Sunday evening service with lecture, and a Thursday evening service followed by séance. One other Church of England clergyman occasionally took part in our services, and I had help from one or two occultists in the way of lectures; but most of the work I did myself, because I had made up my mind to stand or fall by that year's experiences. If the results came out as promised, I should feel bound and fully disposed to go on with the work. If they did not—and I knew from experience how necessary it was to balance alternatives,

—then I should conclude, not that the whole thing was untrue—I was not so illogical—but that, however out of joint the time might be, I was not born to set it right.

Such argumentation, I think, was logical, and I am comfortably assured it was modest. At all events it made me work with a will during the time of probation.

When the witty Canon of St. Paul's suffered from insomnia, according to his own account he used to take one of his own sermons and read it over. It never failed to produce the desired effect—so he assures us in his own sarcastic fashion.

Well, I sometimes take up one of the MSS. of these old mystic oratory addresses and read it, not as an invocation of Sleep, but rather as a memorial tribute to Mnemosyne. It is all over now. The house is let to ordinary tenants, who I daresay never hear any ghostly footfalls, or see shadowy forms flit about in the gloaming.

I am going to do a distinctly dangerous thing. I am going to print one of those oratory addresses for my readers to sleep over or skip, unless they like really to be readers. They will at all events see at what I was aiming, and perhaps the words as I wrote them then will be fresher than they would be if I wrote them now. At all events there is the address in a separate chapter, so that it can be read or skipped without breaking sequence. In the next or concluding chapter I shall tell the outcome of it all, and set down the exact point of the compass by which I am now steering my course towards the Borderland.

CHAPTER XII

THE MEANING OF A MYSTICAL SERVICE

"There is not, in my opinion, a more pleasing and triumphant consideration in religion than that of the perpetual progress which the soul makes towards the perfection of its nature, without ever arriving at a period in it. To look upon the soul as going on from strength to strength; to consider that she is to shine for ever with new accessions of glory and brighten to all eternity; that she will be still adding virtue to virtue, and knowledge to knowledge, carries in it something wonderfully agreeable to that ambition which is natural to the mind of man." —ADDISON.

So far as a man can fairly appraise and estimate his own motives, I believe my object in publishing the following address is an honest desire to give, in the most personal form, the progress of events, and that I am not influenced by any ambition to see my own sermon in print. It can, as I have said, be ruthlessly "skipped" by those who have an intelligent, and to me quite intelligible, objection to this class of literature. I give it word for word as delivered to the faithful few gathered in my "mystic oratory":—

"WHAT MEAN YE BY THIS SERVICE?"
—Exodus xii. 26.

I shall not be at all surprised if, even now, after all I have been saying and doing for these months past, some of you may still feel inclined to quote this text to me, and say, "What do you mean by this service?" The question is a very natural and a very reasonable one; and I shall do my best to answer it fully and frankly. Fully I may not be able to answer it now, because, from its very nature, the question is a large one, and involves many details; but I will at all events answer it frankly.

Why—it may fairly be demanded—have you, an ordained clergyman of the English branch of Christ's Catholic Church, fitted up this private chapel or conventicle—this "Church in the House" as you call it—and asked us to come to it instead of going to evensong in one of the many churches around whose bells have been chiming out to call us thereto? Have you something better than Christianity to offer us? Are you drifting away from the Church of England yourself, and asking us to follow you into some strange country?

Of course I answer both those questions with an emphatic "No." But a negative answer would be quite insufficient; and I will do my best to-night to tell you affirmatively—(1st) what is the attitude of mysticism towards Christianity in general; (2nd) how it stands related to the Church of England, as a branch of the Church Catholic, in particular; and (3rd) lastly, I will point out, so far as time permits, how I propose to render these services supplementary and subsidiary to that Christianity which we all profess, and that Catholic Church to which most of us feel it our privilege to belong.

Glance for one moment again at the text, and take in now along with it the context.

It was the eve of the Exodus. The

Hebrews were going forth to a closer walk with God than had been compatible with their position so far. They were not going to change their God or their faith—the old faith of Abraham and the Patriarchs. They were going to take a forward step, but not to give up anything they had before. The solemn Passover rite was about to be instituted; and they could understand its significance. But Moses foresaw that, in the generations to come, the old meaning might be lost. It might degenerate into a mere form; as Archdeacon Farrar said at the Church Congress, "The service of God has become a thing of words and ceremonies;" and it was against this he provided. "It shall come to pass, when your children shall say unto you, 'What mean ye by this service?' that ye shall say, 'It is the sacrifice of the Lord's Passover.'"

How closely every word of this applies to us—especially that last word—will appear hereafter.

THE MEANING OF A MYSTICAL SERVICE

What do I mean by this service?

Thirty-four years ago I was brought into contact with what I now call mysticism. I do not mean to say I had not before that seen certain phenomena which I could not explain, and which were called by another name. But then for the first time I got an intelligent answer to questions. I asked what was the use of this new revelation—for such it claimed to be; and I got this answer, "It may make men believe in God."

It was a revelation to me. I saw at once that if the facts were true, they placed religion on a new basis: they gave a fresh meaning to the word faith. It was no longer belief at second hand, but conviction based on reasonable evidence.

I wish I could convey to you what a revolution those seven words effected in all my previous modes of thought.

But when I say "revolution," do I mean that it loosened my hold on Christianity?

Surely no. On the contrary, it tightened my grip of the old truths.

True, I saw it had this effect on some. They made this latest -ism a rival to Christianity—made a new religion of it. But could anything be more illogical?

Put the matter thus. Some friend or relation had left you and gone out to a far country (what else have our departed ones done?), and you had faith in the good ship that bore them across the sea, and hope that they were settled in their new home.

By-and-by you got a letter or a cablegram from them to say they *had* arrived safely and *were* happily settled. Would that shake your faith in the good ship? would it not rather confirm it? Would it damp your hope? would it not, on the contrary, turn that hope into certainty? Surely that is a common-sense way of looking at the matter!

Yes, but what do you mean by "the good ship?" some of these illogical people might ask. They did ask it, and they do ask it still.

I reply firmly, I mean the ship of the Church—Christ's Catholic Church—to one branch of which I claim to belong. I mean the English Church, into which I was baptized, as the ark which should carry me across the waves of this troublesome world to the haven where I would be. The Church whereof I was, as a young man, ordained a priest by the imposition of hands.

But where, asked the illogical ones, do you find any sanction in that Church for this new revelation?

Again I answer firmly, In every creed, in every sacrament and ceremony. I lay my hand on the Bible, and I say, "It is written."

Ten years after I was first brought face to face with these new experiences, I met a press-man in Fleet Street—one who had before cared for none of these things—and he startled me by saying, "I am a full believer in Christianity now. I could not accept the Incarnation or the Atonement, but this new light has made it all clear to me."

Knowing the man, as I did, for a clear, bold, hard-headed thinker, this was a confirmation of my own position; a confirmation I needed even then, for I did not jump to my conclusions as the illogical people did.

More than twice ten years have again gone by since that confirmation came to me; and I have seen no reason to recede from the position I had taken up. On the contrary, the more I read the Bible, the more I look into the origins of Christianity, the more deeply I probe into the formularies of the Catholic Church—the more convinced do I become that this new revelation has come "not to destroy but to fulfil."

That, in a few necessarily vague and imperfect words, is the basis on which I am going to work here.

I retain all my old beliefs; I do not relinquish my position as a clergyman of the Church of England, though the illogical people say I ought to, if I would be consistent.

I have this morning officiated at a Church

of England service, and I shall continue to do so whenever I have the opportunity. I feel my own position to be perfectly clear in this respect; and I can only say, if you do not sympathise with such a view, you will not feel at home here.

With regard to our Sunday service clashing with those in church, I would observe that if the majority felt this to be a difficulty, I should be quite content to forego the Sunday service, and to have it on Thursday evening, which I have set aside for the purpose as being the day of the Christian Passover—the Maundy Thursday to our weekly Easter Day.

Do not misunderstand me when I say that I consider the mere chapel services here the least important of the advantages we have secured by getting a private house of our own.

I mean this, that you can get the Church of England services elsewhere; but the other advantages—you of the inner circle know what I mean—you cannot get elsewhere.

I shall always retain the chapel and the

chapel service, because that is the key to my whole position—the combination of mysticism with the Christian services of the Church of England.

If you feel you ought to go to a regular church on Sunday, go by all means. It would be your plain duty to do so. The voice of conscience is sacred. I should ill deserve the name of a *Christian* mystic if I did not acknowledge this.

It would be quite possible, by a little rearrangement, for you to do both—to go to church and to come here.

I could begin a little later than now, give my reading and lecture first, and then have a short benediction service afterwards. That is a matter for future deliberation.

As it is, members of the choir or congregation can go to their church in the morning and come here in the evening. With the modification I speak of, they could go to church both morning and evening and come here afterwards. Or, as I said, I am willing, if it is desired, to transfer the service altogether to Thursday. I do not wish to do this, though it would leave me free to take duty elsewhere.

I only want to put it on record from the very first that our arrangements here are elastic, and can be modified to suit the convenience of those who cast in their lots with us.

Here, of course, and now, I speak only of such matters as concern those who may from time to time attend these services without being regular members of our circle. To the members I shall address myself elsewhere and at another time.

Taking the broad distinction laid down so clearly by the speaker at our last public Sunday evening service, it might be said that we have to provide separately for the Theology and what may be called the Theurgy of our compound system. I do not remember that he used that particular word Theurgy; but it expresses fully all he spoke of as the higher grades of the comprehensive subject with which he dealt.

Theology is, roughly speaking, the talk about divine things; but Theurgy is the *doing* of those divine things.

Here, in chapel, and in presence of those who may without offence, I hope, be termed outsiders, we can only talk. I do not want to disparage this talk. It would be stultifying myself were I to do so. But we mean to do much more than talk here. The talk only represents the lowest round of our ladder. I hope we shall be able to realise Charles Kingsley's words, "*Do* noble things, not dream them."

At all events we have now, for the next few months, what I have for years been trying to get, a clear stage for making my experiment—that experiment, I can scarcely repeat too often, being the combination of Christian mysticism with our old faith and practice, and the reading of the one in the light of the other.

This is the day of small things; and I know that such a condition is a great trial to some persons. They are inclined to repeat something like the old cry, "Can any good thing come out of Nazareth?"

They forget that the great Churches of Rome and England, which they see around them now, all came out of the little Church in the Catacombs, when a few crack-brained enthusiasts, as they were then called, met to carry out their ideas even in a more hole-and-corner fashion than down a back street in a London suburb. *What if history be going to repeat itself again?*

It *is* a great idea. It is not *my* idea, therefore I can say so—I mean the idea of reconciling Faith and Reason: of proving the after-life, and the presence of the Unseen World around us, just as we prove any fact of science. That is the claim of mysticism; and many persons think that this is the cause of its revival amongst us in the present generation.

People are largely swayed by sight and sense, and many stand aloof from religion altogether, because they say religion requires of them to lay aside their common-sense.

If the slightest, most undignified of these facts which we claim to have witnessed *be* a fact, then religion is at once taken down from the pedestal where it has been perhaps unfortunately placed, and is to be judged by the same tests as you apply to the establishment of any fact in science. Is not that, I ask, a great idea? It is not, I repeat, mine; and therefore I can call it a great idea.

My adaptation of it simply refers to my own position—which is, in a certain degree, the position of most of you too.

I say the Bible recognises this method. Nay more, the Catholic Church in general, and the English Church in particular, recognises and approves it.

Those are briefly the lines on which I am working. That is what I mean by this service.

CHAPTER XIII

THE WAVE SUBSIDING

"The seas are quiet, when the winds give o'er;
  So calm are we when passions are no more.
For then we know how vain it was to boast
Of fleeting things so certain to be lost.
Clouds of affection from our younger eyes
Conceal that emptiness which age descries.

The soul's dark cottage, battered and decayed,
Lets in new light through chinks that time has made.
Stronger by weakness, wiser men become,
As they draw near to their eternal home.
Leaving the old, two worlds at once they view
That stand upon the threshold of the new."
        —*Miratur limen Olympi*—VIRG. (Waller).

"NOTHING so difficult," wrote the poet, "as a beginning in poesy — except perhaps an end;" and it is this latter difficulty I find attaching to the plain prose of my present narrative.

I do not mean to say it is hard to "pull up," as the phrase goes, because I felt from the first that my story must be a short one, if it was to be read. I would risk obscurity rather than prolixity, even though

"Brevis esse laboro, obscurus fio."

I might have expanded my narrative indefinitely, but I felt that condensation rather than expansion was desirable; and my difficulty appertains to the conclusion in a logical sense rather than to that ordinary use of the word which makes it synonymous with "the end"—with that often desirable haven of repose for the reader which is embodied in the eloquent dissyllable "finis."

Hitherto I have given the premises of my logical process. How far am I justified in appending the conclusion that flows out from their juxtaposition?

There is the difficulty. What seems to me to be the logical issue may not so strike others. To revert to the language of the schools, I may have been guilty of a false process somewhere which shall have the effect of making the whole argument one huge fallacy. Once more my exceeding modesty and diffidence will, I think, be obvious even to the most carping critic.

But I must not forget that at present even my premises are incomplete.

What was the upshot of "the mystic oratory"? How far did the "intelligences" make good their high promises?

Patiently and persistently did we pray, sing, preach, and "sit." Week after week did "we gather at the river," in the words of the familiar lyric of the séance-room. Everything, we knew, comes to those who wait; and we waited. Did we not wait?

There was, remember, a distinct promise that the departed would come and fill the vacant chairs which we *left* vacant for them. We strained our eyes through the darkness. We listened for the lightest footfall. None came.

Constantly I thought of the beautiful ending of a sermon by Archdeacon Manning, when he was "Archdeacon" Manning and one of ourselves. Picturing the reunion on the other side, he imagined that we might say to those we met there, "What, were you so close to us, and yet we did not see you! There were times when we felt you were near us; but we looked around and saw nothing; we listened, and all was still."

I purposely cite the passage as it ran through my own mind, instead of hunting it up and making a literal quotation from a book. For weeks and months we thus looked around us and saw nothing; we listened, and all was still.

We got the usual messages purporting to come from our own friends who had gone before us; and one clergyman, brother-in-law of a lady in our innermost circle, was particularly voluble in his communications. We were, he assured us, on the right track, and bound to succeed. That was all. The larger promise was not fulfilled. My tenancy expired; the circle broke up, and I never had the heart to re-form it. I never shall now. I felt that year was critical; and it failed.

I am quite ready to believe that the fault lay with me. I cannot imagine better conditions. A small knot of sincere and earnest persons met at regular intervals, and as a religious exercise in the most solemn sense of the words; indeed I have not said openly *how* solemn those Thursday evening assemblies were. We were told to reproduce as closely as we could the conditions of the forty days between the Resurrection and Ascension; and my reading of those conditions was declared to be right. But the promise remained unfulfilled.

That is the first induction I feel forced to make after carefully questioning my long array of facts. Setting aside all incidents where there was the smallest room for doubt, and resting only upon such as I felt to *be* facts, what was the net result? Well, it was wholly disheartening. Not only was it out of all proportion to the time devoted and the labour bestowed, but the promise deliberately given was utterly unfulfilled.

And this I find, on retrospect, to be a characteristic, not only of the critical year which was to be an *annus mirabilis*, but of almost all the years that preceded. Need one write that qualifying word "almost"?

Set down here in regular series we have of course only the crucial events—the successes, if one may so put it. What do they amount to? One could tell them off upon one's fingers. The uneventful "to-morrows and to-morrows and to-morrows" must perforce go unrecorded.

Yet could one, on the other hand, say that nothing had been gained? Supposing *one* incident—such, for example, as that connected with "Minnie"—proved, would it not go far

> "To shame the doctrine of the Sadducee
> And Sophists madly vain of dubious lore?"

One may possibly, without being over-fanciful, trace the vestiges of a law at work in these partial successes and manifold failures, this grain of wheat amongst a bushel of chaff, this strange mixture of truth and fraud. Since the days of Moses the real miracle and the fraudulent imitation have gone together, and the onus of discrimination has been thrown upon the inquirer. It is an open question after all, perhaps, whether the game is worth the candle, and yet, after spending a lifetime in the investigation, one is disposed to ask, with a very strong suspicion of a negative reply, Would one care to have missed the experience? Has it not tightened one's hold on spiritual things, even though all one's expectations have not been realised? Is there a single phase of life in which one's expectations *are* realised to the full?

"That would be scanned."

The Modern Mystery—if one is to harp on that idiotic expression, in order to avoid a question-begging one—is not special in this respect. As Beattie says in the following apposite lines:—

> "So fares the system-building sage,
> Who, plodding on from youth to age,
> Has proved all other reasoners fools,
> And bound all nature by his rules;
> So fares he in that dreadful hour
> When injured truth exerts her power,
> Some new phenomenon to raise,
> Which, bursting on his frighted gaze,
> From its proud summit to the ground
> Proves the whole edifice unsound."

In this respect, perhaps, the good and ill involved in occultism pretty well balance each other; but the dismal fact remains, that it involves going a long way round to get a very few paces in advance, even though the advance be postulated—just as the man in Charles Lamb's essay felt it necessary to burn down his shanty and pig-sties every time he wanted to get a taste of roast pork.

Possibly what we may call "spiritual law in the natural world" proceeds upon this very principle, that all we can compass here must, in the nature of things, be fragmentary and incomplete. In that case the promise of fuller revelation must have been due either to our own exuberant wish or to information purposely fraudulent or unintentionally defective in the "intelligences" who gave it.

As to the religious aspect of the subject, I cannot of course let my readers off without "a few words" on this portion of the matter; "'tis my vocation, Hal." There is a real danger here, as will, I think, have been made apparent from the narrative itself, without requiring anything like homiletic treatment.

The boast of the occultist, as formally enunciated by one of those with whom I have dealt, is "We do not *believe* — we *know*." Theology, from the standpoint of the occultist, is to become as much a fixed science as geology. The idea is very attractive. I am not saying that it is false or fallacious. Some have found it not to be so. They have lived and died by it. But others have not been so fortunate. Their experiments have not succeeded; and then the danger is, not that they will simply give up occultism and go back to the point from which they started, but that all religion will go by the board. That is a real peril which every one must face who goes in for exceptional privileges. If they fail, all is apt to fail. I purposely refrain from dealing with this danger at any length, because I do not wish to give a didactic turn to my narrative. I want to leave it a narrative—to make it an object-lesson from which intelligent readers shall draw their own conclusions.

For the evil results supposed to be inseparable from occultism, in this respect occultists have in a great degree themselves to thank. They have too often introduced an entirely unnecessary antagonism between their own system and all recognised forms of faith and practice. They pose as "pale Galileans," and denounce the advocates of religion as scribes and Pharisees; while churchgoers and chapel-people, instead of being conciliatory, have done their best to widen the breach. This fault seems pretty evenly balanced on both sides.

About the moral and intellectual dangers still less need be said. I believe they are greatly exaggerated. The immorality of dark séances has been hinted at in no obscure terms. I have never seen it. The obvious rejoinder is that of course I could not see in the dark. But I have had ample opportunity of observing, and cannot recall anything approaching a breach of good morals. As to the dangers of hypnotism, M. Teste has a striking chapter in his book on animal magnetism, entitled "On the Necessity of Morality in Magnetisers;" but he says nothing that is not equally applicable to a doctor in consultation with a patient or a lawyer with a client. It is akin to the danger of the confessional. There is always danger where a person's volition is in any degree put into the charge of another.

As to what a distinguished scientist meant when he spoke coarsely of one form of occultism as "intellectual whoredom," I confess I am too innocent to understand. If the designation be a true one, why do not the scientists try to stamp out the system, or at all events to expose it, instead of letting it run riot around them while they sit still in contemptuous silence! This *laches* is as bad as the analogous treatment of the social evil by what is called "Society."

Anyhow one need not be quite so iconoclastic as to endorse the sentiment which Philip James Bailey—himself a spiritualist—puts into the mouth of one of his characters in "Festus." Two of them discourse as follows:—

"WALTER: Do you believe that spirits interfere
    With men, events, or actions anywhere?
CHARLES: Let gold-bagged priests, from Ganges to
    Bermudas,
    The Gospel preach, according to St. Judas;
    It is my opinion, if the truth were known,
    That earth pertains to man and beast alone;
    And neither saint, nor fiend, nor bright nor
    dark angel,
    Between the South Pole and the Port of
    Archangel,
    Have any call, or leave, or will, or power,
    To meddle with a mortal for an hour."

There is one practical consideration—the most practical, £. s. d. consideration of all—connected with this subject, to which I would give a subordinate place in my records. It is this, that if a man indulges to any extent in occultism, he does so at his own proper risk — nay more, with well-nigh moral certainty of personal loss. The loss may be actual pecuniary damage, or, which is often involved therewith, the loss of influence and position. My own experiences have never been so exclusive as to lay me personally open to this danger; and I have carefully avoided those forms of the occult, such as the indiscriminate use of black magic, which I was warned brought disaster in its train; the spirits (such was the theory of my Master) avenging themselves thus for the command that was exercised over them. Anyhow a large number of occultists have unquestionably "come to grief."

There are of course two other explanations of the fact, if fact it be—one occult, the other as material and commonplace as the fact itself. It may be said that, by seeking to pry into the unseen, we claim superior knowledge—knowledge whereto we have no right to aspire—and therefore pay the penalty. The other solution, which is much more likely to find acceptance, is that by our own act and deed we attest our folly, and society takes us at our own valuation. I know not which theory is the true one; but of the fact having a somewhat wide application I have no doubt.

I have before my mind at the present moment two men at least whose writings won them a foremost place in literature, but who are now utterly shelved, though they are still living and capable of work. If I dared give the slightest clue to their names—which of course I must not—I am sure the majority of my readers would endorse the conclusion to which I have come. The generalisation may not be exhaustive, but it is very striking and conclusive so far as it goes. I am positively amazed when I read the press notices each of these men is able to append to successive editions of his works. I know them both personally, and therefore know they are still in possession of the powers the public so fully recognised; yet their names are scarcely known by the present generation, and the men themselves live in the most complete obscurity.

The wave of supernaturalism about which I spoke at the outset, under due protest, is evidently subsiding. I was not aware that the wave-theory, so to say, had been broached when I used the expression, though the imagery involved is obvious enough, and Mr. Haweis put the matter very clearly in one of his outspoken sermons on the subject. He said:—

"It seems to me that the Unseen World breaks through from time to time in sort of rhythmic waves. Each such outflow is instantly encrusted with imposture and legend; and when the outflow is suspended for a time, its very existence is questioned, and its mythical elements amply exposed. Then when years pass without a miracle or prophecy or manifestation, back comes another wave of supernaturalism, and men are convinced for a time, until they lapse into unbelief from the same causes—*the absence of manifestations.* I think we are now (1873) in the midst of such a wave of supernaturalism. I should not wonder if, in a few years, when every one is convinced of the genuine nature of such phenomena and a spiritual world, if not another sign or sound were seen or heard throughout Christendom for centuries. . . .

"It may be that this movement will not pass, that it will be a key in our hands to an abiding revelation. It may be that we shall be able to master those at present unknown laws and imperfectly seen conditions, which will enable us to detain this wave of supernaturalism, just as we have learned to attract and detain at will the lightning. We may utilise it, summon it, and establish firm channels through which those more advanced than we in spiritual progress may be able to help us on and support us. 'Are they not all ministering spirits sent forth to minister unto such as shall be heirs of salvation?' Whatever may turn out to be the use or the truth in this matter, let us be cool and candid and watchful. Let us have no screaming; let us wait and see."

The screamers are, on the one side, those who cry out "Devil, devil!" on every occasion, as the boy in the fable cried out "Wolf!" until nobody heeds them, and perhaps the devil gets the benefit of the scream. On the other side are those who, scared by the unpopularity of occultism and the imputation of folly it brings with it, simply rush off into other eccentricities, and scream, so to say, in a different key.

In the subsidence of the so-called "spiritual" wave, that of theosophy promised to take its place, until the recent exposures of the *Westminster Gazette* proved the Mahatmas to be no whit more reliable than the "dear sperrits," and Mrs. Besant's " Masters" to be certainly inferior to my own.

Twice I sat at the feet of Madame Blavatsky in Lansdowne Road, and enjoyed her Turkey cigarettes, though I could not say so much of what, in the language of Truthful James, I would again call "the subsequent proceedings." The theosophists seemed to be talking over one another's heads; certainly they talked over mine. Of course that might not have been the fault of the theosophical talk—the retort is obvious. Anyhow, so it was. I got through Mr. Sinnett's "Occult World," but when I came to the middle of his "Esoteric Buddhism" I floundered, just as "Isis Unveiled" really unveiled nothing for me, and "The Secret Doctrine" remained secret. The fault, I repeat, is probably in my own perceptive faculties, and the theosophists at present perhaps wisely abstain from anything like a propaganda.

The Society for Psychical Research, again, is doing good work, no doubt; but it has changed its *venue* as compared with the Dialectical Society in the days of which I have been writing. It professes at best a kind of *fin-de-siècle*, up-to-date occultism, which consists rather in levelling down the occult to the standard of the commonplace, than in that reverse process which was the ambitious aim of what used to be called "Modern Spiritualism."

"Thirty years ago," said Professor Sidgwick, in his presidential address to the Society for Psychical Research, in 1882, "it was thought that want of scientific culture was an adequate explanation of the vulgar belief in mesmerism and table-turning. Then, as one man of scientific repute after another came forward with the results of individual investigation, there was a quite ludicrous ingenuity exercised in finding reasons for discrediting his scientific culture. He was said to be an amateur, not a professional; or a specialist without adequate generality of view and training; or a mere discoverer not acquainted with the strict methods of experimental research; or he was not a Fellow of the Royal Society, or if he was it was by an unfortunate accident. Or, again, national distrust came in; it was chiefly in America that these things went on; or, as I was told myself in Germany some years ago, it was only in England, or America, or France, or Italy, or Russia, or some half-educated country, but not in the land of *Geist*. Well, these things are changed now, and though I do not think this kind of argument has quite gone out of use, yet it has on the whole been found more difficult to work; and our obstinately incredulous friends, I think, are now generally content to regard the interest that men of undisputed scientific culture take in these phenomena as an unexplained mystery, like the phenomena themselves.

"Then again," continued Professor Sidgwick, "to turn to a different class of objectors, I think, though I do not wish to overrate the change, that the attitude of the clergy has sensibly altered. A generation ago the investigator of spiritualism was in danger of being assailed by a formidable alliance of scientific orthodoxy and religious orthodoxy; but I think that this alliance is now harder to bring about. Several of the more enlightened clergy and laity who attend to the state of religious evidences have come to feel that the general principles on which incredulous science explains off-hand the evidence for these modern marvels are at least equally cogent against the records of ancient miracles, that the two bodies of evidence must *primâ facie* stand or fall together, or at least must be dealt with by the same methods."

As matter of hard fact, in the latest Proceedings of the Society found in the British Museum, the names of two bishops stand among the vice-presidents, whilst any number of dignified and beneficed clergy, to say nothing of those "feeble folk" the curates, figure among the members and associates.

And now the task I had proposed to myself

is concluded. I have, as my readers will do me the justice to remember, all along disclaimed judicial functions. Having produced my evidence, such as it is, I forbear to direct the jury. I may speculate; and if I did, I should perhaps forecast the verdict as one of "Not proven." But I forbear.

I feel like the old gentleman in the pit who laments the decadence of the drama. That is, I am sensible that my narrative is so far topheavy that it deals more largely with the archæology than with the present phases of the subject. This was inevitable; I will be optimistic enough to imagine that it is also for the best. Theosophy and psychical research are open to everybody's examination; but the early mountings of the supernatural wave are, to a large extent, arcane. It is always more or less difficult to hark back upon old paths which have once been abandoned; and, for some reason or other, folks seem to have dropped out of those ways which were beginning to become fashionable somewhere about the date of the great Exhibition in 1851, and received the stamp of approval under the circumstances narrated in my Parisian experiences of 1856.

Forty years have gone by—or very nearly so—and now when the anxious inquirer wants to find out a reliable medium, or a circle at which he can square his difficulties, and goes down to the ghostly headquarters at 2 Duke Street, Adelphi, Mr. Godfrey, the courteous and intelligent secretary, only imitates echo, and answers, "Where?" "Where shall wisdom be found, and where is the place of understanding?" At best he can but refer the inquirer to a few sparse advertisements in *Light;* and the illumination perhaps is not quite of the character whereof he was in quest.

Let me—as the old writers are so fond of saying—return from this digression, and resume the thread of my narrative, though I resume but to break off for once and all.

In quoting Mr. Earle's sonnet on the

reverse of my half-title, I pleaded guilty to having had a dream. The dream has lasted twice as long as Rip Van Winkle's, and I am by no means sure that I am quite wide awake yet. In fact I feel that the best words with which I can wind up my present narrative are those of Bully Bottom with reference to his Midsummer Night's Dream :—

"I have had a most rare vision. I have had a dream past the wit of man to say what dream it was. Man is but an ass if he go about to expound this dream. Methought I was—there is no man can tell what. Methought I was, and methought I had; but man is but a patched fool if he will offer to say what methought I had. The eye of man hath not heard, the ear of man hath not seen; man's hand is not able to taste, his tongue to conceive, nor his heart to report, what my dream was. I will get Peter Quince to write a ballad of this dream: it shall be called Bottom's Dream—because *it hath no bottom.*"

POSTSCRIPT

My MS. was finished and in the hands of the publisher when I felt constrained to withdraw it, because in the height of last season a Spiritualistic Conference was announced, and I felt it was due, in common fairness to my subject, that I should attend that Conference, so as to give my readers the latest news, not exactly from spirit-land, but from those spirit-circles from which I was more or less an exile, voluntary or involuntary. I might perhaps be wrong in speaking of the wave of supernaturalism as having subsided. It might only be that I myself was—to be true to my metaphor—not "in the swim."

I would at all events complete my narrative—post it up to date—by giving, so far as possible, the *status quo* of spiritualism in the summer of 1895. I use the word "spiritualism" freely now, because I am writing as an outsider.

In the merry month of May, then, when the "Shining Ones," as Charles Lamb called them, throng Exeter Hall for the annual "Meetings," I followed this ghostly Conference, like a devotee, from the opening religious service in St. Andrew's Hall to the final conversazione at the Portman Rooms, at which latter function the fatted calf and the young ladies' fiddles seemed to welcome me like a prodigal son, and to protest against spiritualism being dead. It was surely very much alive.

At the religious service in Newman Street occurred an instance of what really seemed like thought-reading—or occultism.

Remember that the secret of my impending narrative was known only to my publisher, my wife, and myself. I doubt if even either of those two—wife or publisher—remembered the fact that I had, at the conclusion of my experiences, spoken of the "wave" of supernaturalism as subsiding. At the opening of the Conference, the Rev. John Page Hopps preached an excellent sermon on the subject of "Spiritualism, the Key that Unlocks all Doors." He handled the topic dexterously and eloquently, in a manner that quite carried me back to my own old hopeful days in the fifties, and made me feel as uncomfortable as they say a good sermon ought to make one feel. I certainly felt more interested than one sometimes does at the fag-end of a sermon; for, when the peroration came, Mr. Hopps used the following words:—

"So, then, friends, we meet together, strengthened by the knowledge that, pressing hard on the *wave* of agnosticism, there is a *wave* of intensest interest in spiritual subjects, which looks as though it would prevail."

Of course at the bare mention of a wave

I started "like a guilty thing;" and the preacher went on.

"Perhaps the *wave* of mediumship has somewhat abated: I know not; but I do know that the *wave* of spiritual inquiry is mounting higher every day."

It was curious that among all the figures, tropes, and metaphors which were available, he should go floundering about in those "waves." Of course the ordinary critic would set it all down to "coincidence," but my previous experiences would not let me be satisfied with such a theory as that. The preacher must be unconsciously aware of my presence, and, by some occult process, know the lame and impotent conclusion at which my narrative had arrived.

Well, for all those days I haunted that Conference like an unquiet ghost. Some of my old friends and acquaintances who saw me there began to twit me with the couplet:

"On revient toujours
 A ses premiers amours."

Some looked askance at me as though they thought I was a traitor in the camp; but many more did not look at me at all. They were new people, and did not know or care who I was. To them I only represented one of the general public who had strayed, it might be inadvertently, into that mystic circle.

For myself, I felt very much as a *revenant* might feel in coming back to this earthly plane after an æon or so's absence. There were Banquo's chairs everywhere. I missed the old familiar faces at every step; but there were new faces to make up—numerically at all events—for their absence.

The Rev. Page Hopps, to wit, of whose sermon I have spoken, and who seemed to represent the high priest of the cult, was comparatively a new man, and perhaps his position showed the trend of the movement in the direction of free thought—showed, perhaps, after making allowance for difference of individual powers, why my effort in the direction of Anglicanism failed, while his in the direction of Unitarianism succeeded. One would have thought there was room for both; but it was not so.

The new man *par excellence* was, of course, Mr. Stead, whose venture in Borderland has been in every sense a success. I regard the acquisition of this versatile gentleman as a distinct score for spiritualism. His address was far and away the best at the whole Conference, and the very homeliness of his phraseology was a pleasant contrast to the twang—if one may use that word—which marred too much of the other speakers' talk. Speaking, for example, of those to whom I have alluded above, Professor Huxley (then alive) and Mr. Maskelyne, this outspoken advocate of his own new convictions said that he had no particularly idolatrous regard for either of the gentlemen named, but he did recognise them as persons whose word and authority would be recognised as decisive by vast multitudes. "You and I," he proceeded, " cannot go round and convert thirty or forty millions of people all over the country; but if we could convert the bell-wethers of the flock, the flock would follow all right." While therefore he did not regard the scientist and the conjurer with any spirit of idolatrous veneration, he felt that they had to "nobble" these people somehow. But they would never "nobble" them with idle talk. They would have to show them facts, to give them tests, to prove to them that spiritualists were not idle, deluded fools, but men and women with their heads screwed on their shoulders the right way.

There was a charm in that expressive verb "nobble" which carried me, at all events, back to the palmy days of the *Pall Mall Gazette;* and when he went on to quote the directions given by his familiar "Julia" as to the mode of procedure to be adopted for commanding the spirits, I began to wonder whether I had made the most of my forty years in the wilderness, or whether I might not have been, after all, hasty in bringing my *annus mirabilis* to its abrupt conclusion. He had, he said, consulted "Julia" about this procedure, and she had given advice which, if it smacked a little of a ghostly Circumlocution Office, at all events suggested the wholesome doubt as to whether forty years might not be too brief a space for exhausting the details of the Modern Mystery.

He had frequently consulted "Julia" on these matters, and when she had written about it he had said, "What do you wish to be done?" Her reply was, "What you want is mediums — good mediums — not merely good psychics, but mediums who have some care for the cause, and the desire to labour for their fellow-men in their hearts." Supposing you had obtained a supply of good mediums, and some one came to you mourning, broken-hearted, yearning to gain some tidings of some one who had gone before, and of whose fate they felt in utter darkness. You went first to an ordinary clairvoyant, and stated the desire of the bereaved to gain word of the departed. Then let a record be made of what the clairvoyant said, let the description be noted and taken down. Then it was necessary to go from the normal clairvoyant to those psychics who were somewhat further advanced, who were not only clairvoyant but clairaudient, and let them say what they saw and heard as to the identity of the spirit who might appear, allowing no communication whatever between the normal clairvoyant and the clairaudient. Next go to a medium for automatic writing, and ask whether the person whom it is desired to hear from will use the hand of the automatic writer. If a letter is obtained, then go to a medium like David Duguid, and see if you can obtain a photograph of the person. Then a psychographic medium might be consulted—one of those mediums through whom autographs in the direct writing of the departed are obtained —and an effort made to obtain, under test conditions, in locked slates, the signature of the deceased. Then, if there was an approximate agreement in the results obtained through all the mediums, as a final experiment a visit might be paid to a materialising medium, in order to ascertain whether it was possible to get the spirit sought for materialised. Then (so Julia had written) if you do that, and you have the whole range of tests, and they all agree, how much longer do you suppose that people will go about indulging in the old fallacy that dead people are dead and not alive?

Naturally, the two addresses which I was prepared to regard with greatest interest were those which dealt severally with "An Ideal Religious Service," and "The Duty of Spiritualism to the Young." Suffice it to say, I gained nothing from the former which I had not already practically learned from the Rev. John Page Hopps' opening function; and that I cordially agreed with Mr. Stead, who was in the chair, and strongly objected to the unnecessarily destructive character of the latter utterance. The concluding conversazione at the Portman Rooms was a new endorsement of the fact that these spiritualistic folk know how to make the best use of both worlds, in the sense that they can always get a lot of people together, and keep them amused when they do get them. And the people are not the grim fogeys one would expect to meet in the wake of the "spooks," but young folks, men and women of light and leading, whose presence, I am bound to acknowledge, made good the opening remark of the president, Mr. Dawson Rogers, that, whereas Mr. Maskelyne had confidently assured the public that spiritualism was as dead as a door-nail, the success of the Conference ought to effectually refute that assertion.

Whether that event was the final ebb of the wave, or a sign that the tide is beginning to flow again, time alone can show.

9 HART STREET, BLOOMSBURY,
LONDON.

NEW PSYCHIC BOOKS

PUBLISHED BY

Mr. GEORGE REDWAY.

I.

A Handbook of Palmistry after the Ancient Methods. By ROSA BAUGHAN. Sixth (Revised) Edition. With Five Plates. Demy 8vo, 32 pp., paper wrapper. 1s. net.

II.

Anna Kingsford. Her Life, Letters, and Work. By her Collaborator, EDWARD MAITLAND. Illustrated with Portraits, Views, Facsimiles, &c. 2 vols. Demy 8vo, 896 pp., cloth. 31s. 6d. net.

III.

Light on the Path. A Treatise written for the personal use of those who are ignorant of the Eastern wisdom, and who desire to enter within its influence. By M. C. New (Enlarged) Edition, to which is added "Green Leaves." Imperial 32mo, cloth. 2s. net.

IV.

The Story of the Year. A Record of Feasts and Ceremonies. A sequel to "Light on the Path." By M. C. Imperial 32mo, 56 pp., cloth. 2s. net.

V.

A Religion of Law. Being the Conclusions of a Student of Psychic Facts. By V. C. DESERTIS. Crown 8vo, 350 pp., cloth. 5s. net.

On the Evidence of the Senses, Mediumship, the Morality of Spiritualism, Matter and Ether, the Orders of Existence, the Gate of Death, Body the Present Result, Soul the Forming Power, Spirit the Directing Will, the Human Family, &c.

VI.

Miracles and Modern Spiritualism. Three Essays. By ALFRED RUSSELL WALLACE, D.C.L., LL.D., F.R.S. New (Revised) Edition, with Chapters on Phantasms and Apparitions. Crown 8vo, 296 pp., cloth. 5s. net.

VII.

The Great Secret, and its Unfoldment in Occultism. A Record of Forty Years' Experience in the Modern Mystery. By a Church of England Clergyman. Crown 8vo, 320 pp., cloth. 5s. net.

VIII.

Neo-Platonism. Porphyry the Philosopher to his wife, Marcella. Now first Translated into English by ALICE ZIMMERN. With Preface by RICHARD GARNETT, C.B., LL.D. Crown 8vo, cloth. 3s. 6d. net.

IX.

The Gnostics and their Remains, Ancient and Mediæval. By C. W. KING. Second Edition. With Woodcuts and Plates. Royal 8vo, xxiii–466 pp., cloth. 10s. 6d. net (formerly published at 21s.)

X.

The Rationale of Mesmerism. By A. P. SINNETT. Second Edition. Cloth. 2s. 6d. net.

XI.

Complete Translation of La Haute Magie of Eliphas Levi. By General DOUBLEDAY and Dr. ALEXANDER WILDER.

XII.

Experiences of a Clairvoyant. Being the Autobiography of Isabel Wilson (*née* Tilley). Crown 8vo, 160 pp., cloth. 3s. 6d. net.

www.ingramcontent.com/pod-product-compliance
Lightning Source LLC
Chambersburg PA
CBHW030732230426
43667CB00007B/684